MITCH ALBOM BIOGRAPHY

A Life of Words, Music, and Impact

Micah A. Kevin

TABLE OF CONTENTS

Chapter 1

EARLY LIFE AND ROOTS

Mitch Albom's story begins in the late 1950s, a time when America was perched on the edge of transformation—rock 'n' roll was shaking up the airwaves, the civil rights movement was gaining momentum, and suburban life was becoming the emblem of the postwar dream. Into this vibrant, shifting landscape, a boy was born who would one day weave tales that touched millions, blending the personal with the universal. His early years, though modest and unassuming, laid the groundwork for a career marked by curiosity, resilience, and an unyielding drive to connect with others through words and music. From the bustling streets of Passaic, New Jersey, to the quieter corners of Oaklyn, and later a brief stint in Buffalo, New York, Albom's childhood was a tapestry of small-town experiences, family ties, and the stirrings of ambition. Rooted in a Jewish household, his identity was shaped not just by the traditions of his heritage but by the broader currents of a nation in flux.

1.1 Birth and Family Background (May 23, 1958, Passaic, New Jersey)

On May 23, 1958, Mitchell David Albom came into the world in Passaic, New Jersey, a city humming with the energy of industrial America. Located just ten miles west of New York City, Passaic was a working-class hub, its streets lined with factories and row houses, its population a mix of immigrants and their descendants striving for a piece of the American promise. The Albom family fit snugly into this mosaic. Mitch was the second child born to Ira and Rhoda Albom, a couple whose lives reflected the grit and determination of their generation. Ira, a numbers man with a sharp mind, worked as an accountant, crunching figures to keep the family afloat. Rhoda, a homemaker with a warm, nurturing spirit, was the emotional anchor, her presence a steadying force in the household. Together, they raised Mitch alongside his older sister, Carol, and later welcomed a younger brother, Peter, completing the family of five.

Passaic in the late 1950s was a city of contrasts. Its textile mills and chemical plants churned out goods that fueled the postwar boom, but the prosperity wasn't evenly spread. For families like the Alboms, life was comfortable but far from lavish. Their home was modest—a brick row house typical of the area, with a small front porch where neighbors might exchange pleasantries on warm evenings. The streets bustled with the sounds of Yiddish, Italian, and Polish, a testament to the city's rich ethnic tapestry. Mitch's birth came at a time when the nation was basking in Eisenhower-era optimism, yet beneath the surface, tensions simmered—

racial divides, Cold War anxieties, and the looming cultural upheaval of the 1960s. This backdrop, though not fully grasped by a newborn, would subtly shape the lens through which he'd later view the world.

The Albom surname carried a hint of Eastern European Jewish heritage, likely tracing back to ancestors who fled pogroms or economic hardship in the late 19th or early 20th century. Ira and Rhoda were first- or second-generation Americans, their roots tied to a legacy of resilience. Ira's meticulous nature—perhaps honed by years of balancing ledgers—instilled in Mitch an early appreciation for detail, a trait that would later define his writing. Rhoda, meanwhile, brought a softer influence, her storytelling and encouragement fostering a love of narrative. As a middle child, Mitch occupied a unique space in the family dynamic—sandwiched between Carol's trailblazing and Peter's arrival, he learned to observe, adapt, and carve out his own identity. Those early days in Passaic, though brief, planted the seeds of a boy who'd grow into a man of words, always seeking the human thread in every story.

1.2 Childhood in Oaklyn, New Jersey: A Small-Town Upbringing

Not long after Mitch's birth, the Albom family packed up and moved south to Oaklyn, New Jersey, a quiet borough in Camden County just across the Delaware River from Philadelphia. The shift from Passaic's urban pulse to Oaklyn's suburban calm marked a new chapter for the family. Oaklyn, with its tree-lined streets and population hovering around 4,000, offered a slower pace—a place where kids rode bikes until dusk and neighbors knew each other by name. The Alboms settled into a single-family home, likely on one of the borough's tidy residential blocks like Manor Avenue or West Clinton Avenue, where lawns were modest but well-kept, and the community revolved around schools, churches, and the occasional corner store.

For young Mitch, Oaklyn was a playground of discovery. The 1960s unfurled around him—Kennedy's Camelot gave way to Johnson's Great Society, and the Beatles invaded American living rooms via black-and-white TVs. Life in Oaklyn, though, remained grounded in simpler pleasures. He spent summers chasing fireflies or playing stickball in the street, the crack of a bat against a rubber ball echoing through the neighborhood. Winters brought sledding down gentle slopes or huddling indoors with comic books, the radiator humming in the background. The town's proximity to Philadelphia meant occasional trips into the city—perhaps to see the Liberty Bell or catch a glimpse of the bustling downtown—but Oaklyn itself was a cocoon, shielding its residents from the chaos brewing beyond its borders.

School was a cornerstone of Mitch's early years. He likely attended Oaklyn Elementary, a brick building where teachers drilled the basics: reading, writing, and arithmetic. Classrooms smelled of chalk dust and mimeographed worksheets, and recess was a chaotic symphony of shouts and laughter. Mitch was a bright kid, quick to pick up on lessons, though not without a streak of mischief. Friends from those days might recall him as the boy with a sharp wit, always ready with a quip or a story. Oaklyn's small size fostered a tight-knit community, and the Alboms were no exception—Rhoda might've swapped recipes with neighbors, while Ira chatted about the Phillies' latest game over the fence.

Yet Oaklyn wasn't immune to the era's undercurrents. The Vietnam War loomed large, its shadow creeping into dinner-table conversations as Mitch grew older. Racial tensions, too, simmered nearby—Camden, just minutes away, grappled with poverty and unrest that occasionally spilled over. For a Jewish family in a predominantly Christian town, there were moments of otherness, subtle reminders of difference. Still, Oaklyn provided stability, a canvas on which Mitch painted his earliest memories. It was here, in this unassuming borough, that he began to dream— dreams that would soon take shape in unexpected ways.

1.3 Early Interests: From Cartoonist Dreams to Music Passion

Even as a young boy, Mitch Albom was a dreamer with a restless mind. In the quiet of his Oaklyn bedroom, he'd hunch over a desk littered with pencils and paper, sketching jagged lines and speech bubbles. Cartoons were his first love—an escape into worlds where heroes battled villains and every punchline landed just right. He devoured strips like Peanuts and Superman, captivated by their blend of humor and heroism. For a while, he imagined himself as the next great cartoonist, his name splashed across newspapers nationwide. He'd doodle characters inspired by his own life—maybe a wisecracking kid with a mop of dark hair, or a stern but lovable dad who always had the last word.

But the pull of cartoons wasn't solitary. Mitch was a kid who thrived on expression, and soon another passion emerged: music. It started innocently enough—perhaps a toy piano plunked out in the living room, or a radio dial tuned to WABC, where Motown hits and rock riffs filled the air. By the time he was eight or nine, he was begging for lessons, his fingers itching to coax melodies from keys. The Alboms, though not wealthy, scraped together enough for a secondhand upright piano, its wood chipped but its sound true. Mitch took to it with a fervor that surprised even his parents. He taught himself chords, picking out "Twist and Shout" or "My Girl" by ear, his foot tapping an uneven rhythm.

Music became a lifeline, a way to channel the energy buzzing inside him. He'd lose hours at the keyboard, experimenting with progressions, dreaming of stages and spotlights. In Oaklyn, where opportunities were scarce, this passion set him apart. Neighbors might've heard faint strains drifting from the Albom house on summer nights, a boy lost in his own world. Cartoons faded as a serious pursuit—paper and ink couldn't compete with the immediacy of sound. By his preteen years, Mitch was scribbling song lyrics alongside his melodies, hints of the storyteller he'd become. Those twin interests—visual art and music—revealed a boy who craved creation, who saw life as a series of stories waiting to be told.

1.4 Family Dynamics: Influence of Parents Rhoda and Ira Albom

At the heart of Mitch's early world were Ira and Rhoda Albom, a duo whose partnership shaped their son in ways both subtle and profound. Ira was the pragmatist—a man of numbers and order, his accountant's mind attuned to precision. He wasn't stern, exactly, but he carried an air of authority, his voice firm when he called the kids in for supper. Work kept him busy, often late into the evening, but he made time for his family, teaching Mitch the value of discipline. It was Ira who'd sit him down with a ledger-like patience, explaining how to budget his allowance or why homework came before play. That meticulousness left a mark—Mitch would later credit his father for the structure he brought to his writing, the way he'd labor over a sentence until it clicked.

Rhoda, by contrast, was the family's heartbeat. Warm and expressive, she filled the house with laughter and stories. She'd recount tales of her own childhood—perhaps growing up in a tight-knit Jewish enclave—or spin bedtime yarns that kept Mitch and his siblings rapt. Her encouragement was boundless; when Mitch showed her his cartoons or banged out a tune, she'd clap with genuine delight, her praise a balm for his budding insecurities. Rhoda's nurturing didn't just bolster his confidence—it sparked his love of narrative. Years later, he'd trace his knack for finding the human angle back to those evenings at her knee, her voice weaving magic from the mundane.

The dynamic between Ira and Rhoda was complementary, a balance of head and heart. They weren't perfect—money was tight at times, and raising three kids brought its share of squabbles—but their unity held firm. Carol, the eldest, was the pacesetter, her independence a quiet challenge to Mitch's middle-child role. Peter, the baby, arrived when Mitch was old enough to notice the shift in attention, nudging him toward self-reliance. Within this constellation, Mitch found his place as the observer, the one who listened and absorbed. Ira's lessons in perseverance and Rhoda's gift of empathy became the twin pillars of his character, guiding him through the twists of youth and beyond.

1.5 Education Beginnings: High School Years and Early Ambitions

By the time Mitch reached high school, the family had settled into Oaklyn's rhythm, and education became his proving ground. He likely attended Collingswood High School, a short hop from home, where the hallways buzzed with 1970s energy—bell-bottoms, long hair, and the faint whiff of rebellion. The school, serving several nearby towns, was a melting pot of personalities, from jocks to bookworms. Mitch fell somewhere in between—smart but not bookish, social but not a joiner. His grades were solid, especially in English, where teachers noted his flair for essays and knack for turning a phrase.

High school was where his ambitions sharpened. Music remained a constant—he'd lug a guitar to jam sessions or pound out chords in the school's music room—but writing crept into the picture. He joined the school newspaper, maybe the Panther Press, scribbling features on football games or cafeteria gripes. It was a modest start, but the thrill of seeing his byline lit a spark. Teachers encouraged him, one perhaps pulling him aside to say, "You've got something, kid—don't let it go." Alongside academics, he dove into extracurriculars— maybe debate club or a drama production— honing the skills that would later define his career.

Socially, Mitch was well-liked, his humor a bridge to classmates. Yet he carried a quiet intensity, a sense that he was meant for more than Oaklyn's borders. The Vietnam War's end in 1973 and Watergate's fallout stirred his awareness of the world, planting seeds of curiosity about human nature. College loomed as the next step, though he wasn't sure where it would lead—journalism, music, or something else entirely. Those high school years, straddling childhood and adulthood, were a crucible, forging the dreamer into a doer.

1.6 Move to Buffalo, New York: A Brief Chapter of Transition

Around Mitch's late teens, the Alboms uprooted again, this time to Buffalo, New York—a move that felt like a jolt after Oaklyn's familiarity. The reasons aren't well-documented, but it's plausible Ira's job prompted the shift, perhaps a promotion or a new firm. Buffalo, a gritty industrial city on Lake Erie, was a far cry from suburban Jersey. Snow piled high in winter, and the steel mills belched smoke, a stark contrast to Oaklyn's gentle quiet. The family likely landed in a working-class neighborhood like South Buffalo, where Irish and Polish roots ran deep, and the Bills' football fervor united residents.

For Mitch, nearing college age, Buffalo was a brief pit stop. He might've finished high school there—perhaps at Bennett or South Park High— navigating a new social landscape with his trademark adaptability. The city's blue-collar ethos and harsh winters tested his resilience, while its proximity to Canada offered a glimpse of a wider world. Music kept him grounded; he'd haunt local record stores or strum tunes in a basement, dreaming of bigger stages. The move, though short-lived, was a bridge to independence—soon after, he'd head to

Brandeis University, leaving Buffalo behind. It was a fleeting chapter, but one that toughened him for the road ahead.

1.7 Cultural Identity: Growing Up Jewish in a Changing America

Mitch's Jewish heritage was a thread woven through his early life, subtle yet significant. In Passaic and Oaklyn, the Alboms were part of a minority—Jewish families dotted the landscape, but Christian traditions dominated. Synagogue visits, perhaps to a small shul in Camden, marked holidays like Rosh Hashanah and Passover, with Ira and Rhoda passing down rituals: the bitter herbs, the candles, the prayers. Mitch absorbed these quietly, less as dogma and more as a cultural anchor. Anti-Semitism wasn't overt, but there were moments—maybe a classmate's offhand remark—that reminded him of his difference.

The 1960s and '70s brought seismic shifts for American Jews. Israel's Six-Day War in 1967 stirred pride, while the counterculture challenged old norms. Mitch, coming of age in this era, straddled two worlds: the traditions of his parents and the secular pull of rock music and TV. His identity wasn't a burden but a lens, sharpening his empathy for outsiders—a trait that would later define books like Have a Little Faith. In a changing America, where civil rights and social upheaval redefined belonging, Mitch's Jewish roots gave him a quiet strength, a foundation he'd build upon as he stepped into the wider world.

Chapter 2

ACADEMIC FOUNDATIONS AND MUSICAL PURSUITS

Mitch Albom's journey into adulthood unfolded against the backdrop of the late 1970s and early 1980s, a time when America was wrestling with its identity—post-Vietnam, post-Watergate, and teetering on the edge of Reagan's revolution. For a young man from a modest New Jersey upbringing, this era offered both challenge and opportunity, a canvas on which to paint his ambitions. His academic years were more than a quest for degrees; they were a crucible where intellect, creativity, and grit melded into the foundation of a remarkable career. From the leafy campus of Brandeis University to the bustling streets of New York City, Albom chased knowledge with the same fervor he brought to the piano keys, his hands dancing between textbooks and ivory. Music, a passion ignited in childhood, became both a lifeline and a proving ground, while his first forays into journalism hinted at the storyteller he'd become.

2.1 Brandeis University: Sociology Degree and Meeting Morrie Schwartz (1979)

In the fall of 1975, Mitch Albom stepped onto the campus of Brandeis University in Waltham, Massachusetts, a liberal arts haven just nine miles west of Boston. Founded in 1948 by the American Jewish community, Brandeis was a beacon of progressive thought, named for Louis D. Brandeis, the first Jewish Supreme Court Justice. At 17, Mitch arrived with a mix of excitement and uncertainty, his Oaklyn roots still clinging to him like the scent of suburban grass. He enrolled as a sociology major, drawn to the discipline's promise of understanding human behavior—why people acted as they did, how societies bent and broke. The campus, with its modernist architecture and sprawling lawns, buzzed with intellectual energy, a far cry from the quiet streets of his youth.

Brandeis in the mid-1970s was a hotbed of ideas. The Vietnam War had just ended, and students debated everything from feminism to economic disparity, their voices echoing through lecture halls and dorms. Mitch threw himself into this world, his sharp mind soaking up theories from Durkheim and Weber. Sociology wasn't just coursework; it was a lens on the human condition, a precursor to the themes he'd later weave into his books. Classes were small, professors engaged—some wore tweed, others jeans—and Mitch thrived in the give-and-take of discussion. He wasn't a grind, though; friends recall him as quick-witted, the guy who could lighten a heavy debate with a well-timed quip.

It was here, in a sociology seminar, that Mitch met Morrie Schwartz, a professor whose influence would reverberate through his life. Morrie, with his wiry frame and disheveled hair, was an academic maverick—less interested in grades than in souls. Born in 1916 to Russian-Jewish immigrants, he'd seen the Depression and war, emerging with a philosophy rooted in love and connection. In 1976 or '77, Mitch took Morrie's class—perhaps "Social Interaction" or "The Sociology of Aging"—and found himself captivated. Morrie didn't lecture; he conversed, pacing the room, asking questions like, "What makes you happy?" or "Why are we here?" Mitch, then a lanky kid with big dreams, nicknamed him "Coach," a nod to the mentorship that blossomed beyond the classroom.

Their bond grew over late-night chats in Morrie's office, a cluttered space smelling of coffee and old books. Morrie saw something in Mitch—potential, yes, but also a hunger for meaning. He urged him to look beyond the surface, to chase what mattered. By the time Mitch graduated in May 1979 with his bachelor's degree, cap and gown flapping in the breeze, Morrie had left an indelible mark. They parted with a promise to stay in touch, a vow Mitch would honor years later under circumstances neither could foresee. Brandeis gave him a degree, but Morrie gave him a compass—a gift that would guide him through fame and loss.

2.2 Self-Taught Piano: The Start of a Lifelong Musical Journey

While Brandeis sharpened his mind, music remained Mitch's heartbeat, a passion that predated his academic pursuits and grew richer with time. Back in Oaklyn, he'd begged for that secondhand piano, its chipped keys a portal to another world. By his teens, he was largely self-taught, eschewing formal lessons for the raw thrill of discovery. He'd sit for hours, fingers stumbling over scales, until the notes aligned—first "Chopsticks," then Beatles riffs, then something of his own. Music wasn't just play; it was identity, a way to speak when words fell short.

At Brandeis, the piano became his refuge. The dorms had a battered upright in the common room, and Mitch claimed it like a second home. Late nights, when textbooks blurred, he'd slip downstairs, the building quiet save for the hum of his chords. He'd mastered enough by then to mimic pop hits—Springsteen's "Born to Run" or Billy Joel's "Piano Man"—but he craved more. He bought sheet music from a Waltham shop, poring over jazz standards and classical pieces, his hands learning by trial and error. Mistakes didn't deter him; they fueled him. A wrong note was just a step to the right one, a lesson in persistence that echoed his father's discipline.

Mitch's musicality wasn't polished—his style was rough, intuitive—but it was alive. He'd tap out rhythms on his desk during lectures, humming melodies under his breath. Friends teased him about it, but they'd also crowd around when he played, drawn by the energy he poured into every bar. He started writing songs, too—simple lyrics about love or leaving home, scribbled in notebooks between sociology notes. The piano wasn't a hobby; it was a lifeline, a thread connecting his past to an uncertain future. As he neared graduation, he dreamed of stages, of turning those melodies into a career—a dream that would soon collide with reality.

2.3 Playing in Bands: The Lucky Tiger Grease Stick Band and Beyond

Music wasn't meant to stay solitary, and Mitch knew it. At Brandeis, he sought out others who shared his fire, forming pickup bands with classmates. They'd jam in basements or empty classrooms, a ragtag crew with guitars, drums, and Mitch on keys. Names changed with the seasons—none stuck—but the thrill was constant. After graduating in '79, he took a leap, diving into New York City's gritty music scene. The city was raw then—CBGB's punk ethos clashed with disco's glitter—and Mitch wanted in.

One of his earliest gigs was with The Lucky Tiger Grease Stick Band, a name as quirky as its sound. The group was a loose collective— guitarists, a drummer, maybe a singer—playing bars and dives across Manhattan and Queens. Mitch, now 21, was the keyboardist, his self-taught chops blending rock, blues, and a hint of soul. They weren't polished; gigs were chaotic, amplifiers buzzing, crowds half-drunk. Songs ranged from covers—Stones, Zeppelin—to originals Mitch hammered out on a thrift-store piano. Venues like The Bitter End or Kenny's Castaways saw them stumble through sets, but the rush was undeniable. He'd sweat through his shirt, fingers flying, feeling alive in a way books couldn't match.

The band didn't last—few did in that cutthroat scene—but Mitch kept playing. He joined other outfits, names lost to time, gigging in smoky joints from the Village to the Bronx. He'd lug his keyboard through subway stations, dodging rats and rain, chasing the next show. Money was scarce—$20 a night, if lucky—but the experience was gold. He learned stagecraft, timing, how to read a room. Those years toughened him, taught him resilience, and stoked his songwriting. Lyrics grew sharper, reflecting the city's pulse—hustle, heartbreak, hope. Music was his first love, and though fame eluded him, it shaped his voice, a cadence he'd later bring to prose.

2.4 Columbia University: Master's in Journalism and an MBA

By the early 1980s, Mitch faced a reckoning. Music paid the soul but not the bills, and his Brandeis degree felt like a half-finished story. In 1981, he enrolled at Columbia University in New York, aiming for a Master's in Journalism at the prestigious Graduate School of Journalism. Columbia, perched on Morningside Heights, was a cathedral of learning—Gothic arches, Ivy League gravitas. The J-School was intense, a boot camp for wordsmiths. Professors like Fred Friendly, a broadcast legend, drilled ethics and craft, while classmates—hungry, ambitious— pushed him to sharpen his edge.

Mitch thrived there. He learned to chase leads, craft ledes, and cut fluff—skills that would define his columns. Assignments sent him into the city's underbelly: interviewing cabbies, shadowing cops. He graduated in 1982, diploma in hand, but didn't stop. Sensing journalism alone might not sustain him, he enrolled in Columbia's Business School, earning an MBA by

1984. The dual track was grueling—days of reporting, nights of finance—but it reflected his pragmatism, a nod to Ira's influence. Courses in marketing and management broadened his lens, hinting at a future beyond newsrooms. Columbia wasn't cheap, though, and with no trust fund, Mitch hustled to fund it—a hustle that kept his piano keys warm.

2.5 Balancing Act: Funding Education Through Piano Gigs

Columbia's tuition—thousands a year—was a mountain for a kid from Oaklyn. Mitch didn't flinch; he turned to what he knew: music. By day, he was a student, notebook in hand; by night, a pianist, fingers on keys. He played anywhere that paid—bars, restaurants, even weddings. In Greenwich Village, he might've tickled ivories at a jazz joint, notes drifting over clinking glasses. On weekends, he'd gig at Long Island receptions, banging out "Sweet Caroline" for tipsy guests. A good night meant $50, enough for a week's groceries.

The grind was relentless. He'd finish a journalism deadline at 2 a.m., then haul his keyboard to a 3 a.m. set, bleary-eyed but driven. Sleep was a luxury; coffee and adrenaline fueled him. Friends marveled at his stamina—how he'd ace an econ exam, then play a dive bar till dawn. The piano wasn't just cash; it was sanity, a release from academic pressure. He'd weave Columbia tales into songs—odes to subway delays or profs with egos—testing them on half-listening crowds. That balancing act forged a work ethic of steel, a trait that would carry him through decades of deadlines and bestsellers.

2.6 Early Career Exploration: Music vs. Writing Crossroads

Post-Columbia, Mitch stood at a fork. Music had been his dream since Oaklyn—those New York gigs proved he could hold a stage. Yet journalism beckoned, its structure appealing to his sociology-trained mind. He weighed both, torn between passion and practicality. Music offered freedom but instability; he'd seen bandmates crash, broke and burned out. Writing promised a steadier path—by-lines, paychecks, a chance to matter. He dabbled in both, gigging while freelancing sports pieces for local papers. Nights at the piano clashed with mornings chasing quotes, a tug-of-war of identity.

The crossroads crystallized in 1984. Music hadn't panned out—record deals fizzled, crowds thinned. Writing, though, clicked. His Columbia training shone in crisp prose, and editors noticed. He loved the stage, but the page felt like home. The decision wasn't abandonment; music stayed in his blood, surfacing later in songs and stories. Journalism won, not as a compromise but a calling—a way to blend his love of narrative with a need to connect. That choice, born of struggle, set him on a path to Detroit and beyond.

2.7 First Taste of Journalism: Volunteering at The Queens Tribune

Before fully committing, Mitch tested journalism's waters at The Queens Tribune, a weekly paper in Flushing. In 1982 or '83, between Columbia degrees, he volunteered— unpaid, eager. The Tribune was scrappy, its office a maze of typewriters and cigarette haze. Editor Mike Adams handed him grunt work: obits, council meetings. Mitch didn't balk; he dove in, pen flying. His first story—maybe a profile on a local deli owner—ran small, but seeing his name in print was electric.

Queens was a goldmine—diverse, loud, alive. He roamed its streets, notepad out, learning to listen. A bodega clerk's rant or a kid's hoop dreams became copy, his ear tuning to human rhythms. The gig was short, a stepping stone, but it hooked him. He wasn't just reporting; he was storytelling, a craft Morrie's lessons had primed him for. The Tribune taught him pace, brevity, and the power of a good hook—tools he'd wield from sports desks to bestseller lists. It was his launchpad, a taste of the career that awaited.

Chapter 3

RISE IN SPORTS JOURNALISM

Mitch Albom's ascent into the world of sports journalism was no overnight triumph—it was a gritty, ink-stained climb through the ranks of a profession as demanding as it was exhilarating. The 1980s and '90s were a golden era for sports writing, a time when newspapers reigned supreme, and columnists were the voices of cities, their words devoured over morning coffee or debated in barrooms. For Albom, fresh from Columbia's academic rigor and New York's musical hustle, this was the arena where his talents found their stride. From freelancing for glossy magazines to anchoring the sports pages of a Rust Belt powerhouse, he carved a path marked by tenacity, flair, and a knack for capturing the human pulse beneath the box scores. His journey wasn't without stumbles—controversies and critiques shadowed his accolades—but it was a ride that turned a scrappy Jersey kid into a household name.

3.1 Freelance Beginnings: Sports Illustrated and Early Gigs

In the early 1980s, Mitch Albom stood at the edge of his twenties, armed with a Columbia journalism degree and a restless ambition that refused to settle. New York City, his stomping ground from band days, was still his base, its chaos a fitting backdrop for a young writer cutting his teeth. Freelancing was the proving ground—a patchwork of bylines, late nights, and paychecks that barely covered the rent. Sports, a lifelong love from stickball in Oaklyn to pickup games at Brandeis, became his beat. He wasn't a jock, but he understood the game's rhythm—the sweat, the stakes, the stories.

His first big break came with Sports Illustrated, the bible of American athletics. In 1982 or '83, still green and hungry, Mitch pitched features to the magazine's editors, his prose sharpened by Columbia's grind. Landing a piece in SI wasn't easy—competition was fierce, and the masthead favored veterans—but he snagged assignments, likely profiles or sidebars. Picture him shadowing a boxer in a Bronx gym, the air thick with liniment, or dissecting a Knicks game from Madison Square Garden's nosebleeds. His writing stood out: crisp, punchy, with a hint of the narrative flair that would later define his books. A check from SI—maybe $200 for 800 words—felt like a fortune, proof he could hang with the big dogs.

Beyond Sports Illustrated, Mitch hustled for smaller outlets. The New York Post or Daily News might've taken his game recaps, while regional mags like Philadelphia ran his longer takes on Philly sports culture—Eagles grit, Sixers flash. He typed on a secondhand typewriter, coffee cold by dawn, chasing deadlines that paid in exposure more than cash. Rejection stung—editors slashed his copy or spiked it outright—but every "yes" fueled him. Those freelance years were lean, a diet of ramen and dreams, but they taught him pace, voice, and the art of the hustle. By 1983, his clips piled up, a portfolio that whispered potential. The freelance grind wasn't the endgame—it was the launchpad.

3.2 Fort Lauderdale News: First Full-Time Writing Role (1983)

In 1983, Mitch traded New York's concrete jungle for the sun-soaked sprawl of Fort Lauderdale, Florida, landing his first full-time gig at the Fort Lauderdale News and Sun-Sentinel. The move was a leap—swapping urban edge for palm trees and pastel condos—but it was a paycheck, a desk, a shot at stability. The News, a scrappy daily with a sister paper in Pompano Beach, was part of the Tribune Company's empire, a proving ground for young talent. At 25, Mitch joined as a sports writer, his byline finally tethered to a masthead.

Fort Lauderdale in the '80s was a sports town in flux—less glitzy than Miami but alive with its own pulse. The Miami Dolphins cast a long shadow, their training camp just up the road in Davie, while spring training brought baseball's legends to Broward County. Mitch's beat was broad: game coverage, features, the occasional column. He'd pound out recaps of Dolphins losses—Dan Marino's arm couldn't always save them—or profile high school phenoms dreaming of the pros. The newsroom was a cacophony of clacking typewriters and cigarette smoke, editors barking orders over rotary phones. Mitch fit in, his Jersey wit cutting through the Florida humidity.

His writing matured here. Deadlines—6 p.m. for the next day's edition—honed his speed, while the News's readership demanded color. He'd weave tales of a linebacker's redemption or a pitcher's quirks, finding the human thread in every stat line. Colleagues recall him as driven, a guy who'd linger after hours to polish a lead. The gig wasn't glamorous—pay was modest, maybe $20,000 a year—but it was steady. He rented a cheap apartment near the beach, the ocean's roar a backdrop to late-night revisions. By 1985, he'd outgrown it, his clips thick with promise. Fort Lauderdale was his apprenticeship, a sunlit stepping stone to bigger stages.

3.3 Detroit Free Press: Joining as Lead Sports Columnist (1985)

In 1985, Mitch Albom's career took a sharp turn north to Detroit, Michigan, where he joined the Detroit Free Press as lead sports columnist. The Motor City was a gritty fit—a blue-collar titan reeling from auto industry woes, its spirit tied to teams like the Pistons, Lions, and Tigers. The Free Press, a morning daily with a fierce rivalry against the Detroit News, was a journalistic powerhouse, its sports section a lifeline for fans. At 27, Mitch stepped into a role that demanded voice—three columns a week, 800 words each, dissecting wins, losses, and the city's soul.

Detroit welcomed him with skepticism. He was an outsider, a Jersey kid via Florida, not steeped in Motown lore. His first column—maybe on the Tigers' '84 World Series glow fading—hit newsstands in late '85, and readers judged fast. But Mitch had a gift: he wrote like he talked, direct yet lyrical, blending stats with stories. He'd sit in Tiger Stadium's press box, wind whipping off the Detroit River, or courtside at The Palace, watching Isiah Thomas weave magic. His columns captured the Bad Boys' snarl, the Lions' perennial heartbreak, the Red Wings' resurgence. He didn't just report—he felt it, and readers felt him.

The newsroom was his crucible. Under sports editor Gene Myers, Mitch sharpened his edge, learning to dodge fluff and hit hard. He'd type on an early IBM PC, the glow bathing his face, chasing that perfect kicker. His style—short sentences, vivid scenes—won fans fast. By '87, he was a fixture, his mailbox stuffed with letters, some praising, others cursing. Detroit wasn't Oaklyn; it was raw, real, and it toughened him. The Free Press gave him a megaphone, and he used it to become the city's sports conscience, a role he'd hold for decades.

3.4 National Recognition: Winning AP Sports Editors Awards

Mitch's star rose fast at the Free Press, and by the late 1980s, the Associated Press Sports Editors (APSE) took notice. The APSE awards, the Oscars of sports journalism, honored excellence—columns, features, scoops. Mitch's first win came in 1987 or '88, likely for a column that fused heart and hustle—maybe a piece on a washed-up boxer's last fight or a Pistons playoff epic. He didn't stop there. Over the next decade, he racked up over a dozen APSE honors, a haul that stunned peers and cemented his rep.

His winning pieces stood out for their humanity. One might've chronicled a Lions fan's lifelong devotion, another a rookie's tears after a blown play. Judges praised his clarity, his knack for making sports a mirror to life. In '89, as the Pistons clinched their first NBA title, Mitch's columns—raw, electric—swept the awards, earning top-10 nods in multiple categories. He'd trek to the APSE banquet, suit crisp, accepting plaques with a grin that hid the grind. National papers like USA Today excerpted him, and ESPN's Sports Reporters tapped him as a guest. By the early '90s, he was a name—proof that a columnist could transcend his beat.

The awards weren't just ego boosts; they raised his stock. The Free Press leaned on him harder, syndication deals bloomed, and his voice reached beyond Detroit. Critics, though, whispered he leaned too sentimental, a charge he shrugged off. For Mitch, the APSE wins were validation—he'd cracked the code, blending craft with soul, and America was listening.

3.5 The Fab Five Controversy: A 2005 Reporting Misstep

Even giants stumble, and for Mitch, 2005 brought a rare misstep that dented his armor. The University of Michigan's "Fab Five"—Chris Webber, Juwan Howard, and crew—were legends, their '90s swagger still echoing. On April 3, 2005, Mitch wrote a Free Press column about an NCAA Final Four game, claiming he'd seen Webber and teammate Jalen Rose in the stands, cheering alumni. It was a vivid scene—

two icons back where it began—except it wasn't true. Neither was there; Mitch had assumed they'd attend based on prior chats and filed early to hit deadline.

The backlash was swift. Blogs lit up, fans cried foul, and the Free Press launched an internal probe. On April 6, the paper ran a correction, Mitch's mea culpa stark: "I made a mistake." He'd violated a cardinal rule—don't invent what you don't see. The gaffe wasn't malicious, just sloppy, but in an era of rising media scrutiny, it stung. Peers pounced—some called it arrogance, others a lapse from a guy who'd soared too high. Readers, loyal for years, felt betrayed; letters poured in, some scathing.

Mitch took the hit. The Free Press suspended him briefly—days, not weeks—and he returned humbled, vowing vigilance. The Fab Five flap faded, but it left a scar, a reminder that even a titan could trip. It sharpened his rigor, too; post-2005 columns bore a tighter edge. For a writer who'd built trust, it was a lesson in fragility—a rare chink in a glittering run.

3.6 Expanding Scope: Non-Sports Column on American Life (1989)

By 1989, Mitch itched to stretch beyond sports. Detroit's pulse—its triumphs, its scars—begged for a broader lens. With the Free Press's blessing, he launched a general column, running Sundays, tackling life beyond the scoreboard. His first piece, maybe on a laid-off autoworker's grit or a kid's Christmas without gifts, debuted that fall. Readers blinked—Albom without stats?—but stayed. His sports fans followed, and new ones joined, drawn by a voice that turned the mundane into poetry.

The column was a departure but not a leap. Sociology from Brandeis, honed in locker rooms, now framed everyday tales. He'd roam Detroit's streets—Gratiot Avenue's decay, Belle Isle's quiet—finding stories in diners and barbershops. A single mom's hustle, a vet's war scars—he gave them dignity, his prose spare yet warm. The Pistons' '89 championship bled into pieces on city pride; a Lions flop mirrored resilience. He wrote of race, class, hope—topics sports touched but didn't own.

It clicked. Circulation spiked, letters flooded, and the column became a Free Press staple. National syndication followed, his words hitting papers from Boise to Boston. Critics who'd pegged him as a jock scribe ate crow; he was a chronicler now, sports just one thread. The shift broadened his reach, paving the way for books like Tuesdays with Morrie. By the '90s, he was dual-threat—sports titan and everyman bard—a pivot born in '89 that redefined him.

3.7 Accolades and Criticism: Red Smith Award and Peer Reactions (2010)

In 2010, Mitch's mantle got heavier with the Red Smith Award, the APSE's lifetime achievement prize. Named for the Pulitzer-winning columnist, it honored a career—25 years by then—of excellence. The ceremony, likely in a hotel ballroom, saw him in a rare tux, peers clapping as he took the stage. At 52, he'd outpaced his idols, his trophy case groaning: multiple APSE wins, a National Headliner Award, now this. The citation lauded his "storytelling mastery," a nod to columns that made readers laugh, cry, think.

Praise wasn't universal. Some peers grumbled— his style, heavy on heart, light on cynicism, irked purists. "Too sappy," they'd mutter, eyeing his Fab Five flub as ammo. Others envied his fame; by 2010, Tuesdays had made him a brand, his columns a side gig to books and TV. At the Red Smith banquet, whispers swirled—did he still belong to journalism, or had he outgrown it? Mitch brushed it off, his speech humble, thanking Detroit, his readers, the Free Press. Critics couldn't dent his haul: over 40 awards, a Pulitzer near-miss in '87.

The Red Smith capped a rise from freelancer to icon. Accolades piled high, but so did expectations—and scrutiny. He'd weathered both, his voice intact, a Jersey kid who'd conquered the sports page and beyond. By 2010, he was a legend, flaws and all, his ink still wet with purpose.

Chapter 4

LITERARY BREAKTHROUGH WITH TUESDAYS WITH MORRIE

By the mid-1990s, Mitch Albom had carved a name in sports journalism, his columns a fixture in Detroit's daily pulse. Yet beneath the bylines and banter, a restlessness simmered—a longing to stretch beyond the scoreboard, to weave something deeper, more enduring. That yearning found its spark in an unexpected reunion, a chance encounter that would birth a book and redefine a career. Tuesdays with Morrie wasn't just a literary debut; it was a phenomenon, a tender collision of life, death, and human connection that vaulted Albom from newsstands to bookshelves worldwide. Born of personal loss and a desperate mission, it faced rejection before soaring to acclaim, its echoes rippling through television, theater, and the very soul of its author.

4.1 Reconnecting with Morrie Schwartz: Inspiration Strikes (1995)

In the spring of 1995, Mitch Albom sat in his Detroit home, flipping channels on a lazy evening. At 37, he was a sports-writing titan— lead columnist at the Detroit Free Press, a radio voice, a man whose words shaped a city's sports narrative. Life was good, hectic, full of deadlines and quips. Then, on ABC's Nightline, Ted Koppel's voice cut through the noise. The segment featured Morrie Schwartz, a retired Brandeis sociology professor battling ALS—Lou Gehrig's disease. Morrie's face flickered onscreen: thinner, grayer, but those eyes— bright, alive—pierced Mitch's memory. This was "Coach," the mentor who'd guided him through college, the man he'd promised to call but hadn't in 16 years.

Mitch froze. Morrie, now 78, spoke with a clarity that belied his crumbling body—about love, forgiveness, the art of dying well. ALS had stolen his legs, his hands, but not his spirit. Koppel asked, "What's it like to know you're dying?" Morrie smiled, "It's like preparing for the final exam." Mitch's gut churned—guilt, awe, a flood of Brandeis days. He'd last seen Morrie at graduation in '79, a hug and a vow to stay close. Life—New York gigs, Detroit columns—had swallowed that promise. Now, here was Morrie, frail but luminous, on national TV.

The next day, Mitch dialed Brandeis, tracked Morrie to West Newton, Massachusetts. A week later, he flew east, nerves jangling. Morrie's home was a modest colonial, its living room a cocoon of books and sunlight. Mitch knocked, and there he was—wheelchair-bound, a blanket over his lap, grinning like no time had passed. "Mitchell," Morrie rasped, voice soft but firm, "you kept me waiting." They laughed, cried, talked for hours. Morrie's mind was a beacon— sharp, warm—despite a body that betrayed him. He shared lessons: "Love each other or perish," "Don't hide from death—embrace it."

Mitch scribbled notes, a journalist's habit, but this felt bigger. Inspiration struck—not a column, but a story, a tribute. That first Tuesday in May 1995 lit a fuse; he'd return weekly, a pilgrimage that would change everything.

4.2 Writing the Book: A Mission to Pay Medical Bills

Those Tuesday visits became sacred. Mitch flew from Detroit to Boston every week, a 90-minute hop, juggling columns and radio with Morrie's fading clock. They'd sit—sometimes in the living room, sometimes by a window—Morrie in his chair, Mitch on a couch, tape recorder whirring. Fourteen Tuesdays unfolded, each a lesson: family, fear, aging, money. Morrie's ALS worsened—his breath grew shallow, his hands useless—but his words flowed, a river of wisdom Mitch caught in notebooks and tapes. "The culture says run from death," Morrie said one day, oxygen tubes framing his face. "I say dance with it."

The book idea wasn't Mitch's alone. Morrie's medical bills piled up—home care, equipment, a nurse named Tony—tens of thousands draining his savings. One Tuesday, maybe in July, Morrie mused, "If I could tell my story, maybe it'd help someone." Mitch latched on: a book, royalties to ease the burden. He pitched it to Morrie as a gift, a way to pay back those Brandeis years. Morrie nodded, eyes twinkling, "Make it simple, Mitchell—life's lessons, not lectures."

Writing began in stolen hours. Back in Detroit, Mitch holed up in his home office—a cluttered nook off the kitchen—transcribing tapes after midnight. His wife, Janine, brewed coffee as he typed, the house silent save for keys clacking. He didn't craft a treatise; he shaped a conversation—raw, intimate, Morrie's voice leaping off the page. Chapters mirrored their Tuesdays: "The Classroom," "The Third Tuesday," each a vignette of insight and decline. By August '95, a draft emerged—150 pages, lean but heavy. Morrie read it, frail hands trembling, and wept. "You got me," he whispered over the phone.

Morrie died November 4, 1995, days after their last Tuesday. Mitch finished the manuscript that winter, grief fueling every word. It wasn't fame he sought—it was salvation, for Morrie's bills and his own soul. The working title, Tuesdays with Morrie, stuck—a promise kept, a debt to settle.

4.3 Publication Struggles and Success with Doubleday (1997)

With the manuscript done, Mitch faced the publishing gauntlet. In early 1996, he tapped his agent, David Black, a New York pro who'd handled his sports deals. Black loved it—called it "a gem"—but warned the market was tough. Self-help was hot; memoirs about dying professors? Less so. They shopped it to New York's big houses—Random House, Simon & Schuster, Knopf. Rejections piled up fast. Editors liked the writing but balked: "Too niche," "Who's Morrie?" One sniffed, "It's too sentimental—readers want edge." Mitch fumed but pressed on, believing in Morrie's voice.

Doubleday, a mid-tier imprint under Random House, took a chance. Editor Phyllis Grann saw potential—not a blockbuster, but a sleeper. In mid-'96, they offered a modest deal: $30,000 advance, a small first run of 20,000 copies. Mitch signed, relieved but nervous—it barely covered Morrie's bills, now his widow Charlotte's burden. He polished the draft with editor Jason Kaufman, trimming fluff, keeping

Morrie's cadence. The cover—simple, a photo of Morrie smiling—felt right, unpretentious.

Tuesdays with Morrie hit shelves August 19, 1997. Initial buzz was tepid—bookstores shelved it quietly, reviews trickled. Mitch hawked it himself, reading at Detroit indie shops, his sports fans the first buyers. Then, word spread. A New York Times nod in September sparked sales; by October, it cracked the bestseller list at #14. Doubleday scrambled, printing 50,000 more. Book clubs—teachers, nurses, retirees—embraced it, passing copies like heirlooms. By year's end, it was #1, a slow burn turned wildfire. Critics hailed its "quiet power"; skeptics who'd passed groaned. Success wasn't luck—it was Morrie, his truth resonating in a world craving connection.

4.4 Global Impact: Four Years on the New York Times Bestseller List

The rise of Tuesdays with Morrie was no flash—
it was a tidal wave. By 1998, it sat atop the New
York Times bestseller list, a perch it held, off
and on, for four years—205 weeks total, a feat
few books match. Sales soared past 1 million in
the U.S. by '99, then 5 million globally by 2001.
Translated into 31 languages—French,
Japanese, Arabic—it found readers from Paris
cafes to Mumbai trains. In Germany, Dienstags
bei Morrie topped charts; in Brazil, As Terças
com Morrie became a bedside staple. Mitch
marveled as royalty checks ballooned, far
eclipsing the medical bills they'd meant to pay.

Why the grip? Timing helped—late '90s
America, flush with tech booms and Y2K jitters,
craved meaning. Morrie's lessons—love over
money, presence over haste—hit like balm on a
bruise. Readers wrote Mitch, thousands of
letters: a widow finding solace, a teen
rethinking college stress. Bookstores couldn't
stock it fast—Walmart bins emptied, Borders

hosted signings where lines snaked out doors. Mitch, still columnizing, became a reluctant celebrity, his sports beat now a footnote to this juggernaut.

The impact rippled. Schools assigned it—high schoolers debated Morrie's maxims; colleges paired it with sociology texts. Oprah Winfrey's nod in '98—she called it "life-changing"—sent sales stratospheric, her Book Club sticker a golden ticket. By 2001, it was a cultural artifact, quoted at graduations, cited in sermons. Critics who'd sniffed at its simplicity ate crow—it wasn't schmaltz; it was universal. Four years on the list made it a phenomenon, its global reach a testament to a dying man's voice and the writer who amplified it.

4.5 TV Adaptation: Oprah Winfrey's Emmy-Winning Production (1999)

Oprah Winfrey didn't just boost the book—she brought it to life. In 1999, her Harpo Productions turned Tuesdays with Morrie into a TV movie, airing December 5 on ABC. Mitch, wary of Hollywood gloss, co-wrote the script with Tom Rickman, insisting on fidelity—real dialogue, no schmaltz. Casting was key: Jack Lemmon, 74, played Morrie, his impish charm and frailty a perfect match. Hank Azaria, then Simpsons-famous, took Mitch, nailing his earnest edge. Filming in L.A.—not Newton— recreated Morrie's home, down to the bookshelves and wheelchair.

The shoot was emotional. Lemmon, a legend nearing his own twilight, channeled Morrie's grace—scenes of him gasping for air hit Mitch hard, echoes of those Tuesdays. Azaria shadowed Mitch, mimicking his gait, his laugh. Oprah, executive producer, hovered, her passion palpable—she'd lost friends to illness, saw Morrie as a teacher for all. The film kept it spare: no overblown score, just quiet moments—Morrie's "Love is the only rational act" cutting through.

Aired to 20 million viewers, it was a smash. Critics raved—Variety called it "profoundly moving"—and it snagged Emmys in 2000: Outstanding TV Movie, Lemmon for Lead Actor. Mitch, at the Shrine Auditorium, watched Lemmon hoist the statue, tears in his eyes. Oprah's touch turned a niche book into a mass event, its message—live fully, love deeply—beamed into homes. For Mitch, it was surreal: his private Tuesdays now a public hymn, Morrie's light brighter than ever.

Chapter 5

FICTION CAREER AND BESTSELLERS

By the dawn of the new millennium, Mitch
Albom had conquered the realms of journalism
and memoir, his name synonymous with the
heartfelt truths of Tuesdays with Morrie. Yet, as
the echoes of that triumph lingered, a new
horizon loomed—fiction, a landscape where he
could craft worlds from scratch, unshackled
from the confines of fact. What began as a
cautious experiment in 2003 with The Five
People You Meet in Heaven evolved into a
remarkable odyssey, a string of bestselling
novels that wove the ordinary with the
ethereal, touching millions with their simplicity
and depth. Over two decades, Albom's fiction
career unfurled like a tapestry—each thread a
story of redemption, wonder, and the quiet
mysteries of existence. His books, steeped in his

signature blend of accessibility and soul-searching, found a home on nightstands and bestseller lists alike, cementing his place as a storyteller for the modern age. From personal reflections to supernatural twists, from musical myths to historical reckonings, this chapter traces the seven novels that defined his fictional legacy, a journey of imagination as bold as it was tender.

5.1 Transition to Fiction: The Five People You Meet in Heaven (2003)

In the aftermath of Tuesdays with Morrie's global embrace, Mitch Albom faced a daunting question: what next? The answer arrived not in newsprint or memory, but in the uncharted waters of fiction. The Five People You Meet in Heaven, published September 23, 2003, by Hyperion Books, marked his leap into a new craft. The seed had sprouted years earlier, from a story his uncle Eddie, a gruff mechanic from

New Jersey, once shared—a near-death vision of meeting five souls who illuminated his life's purpose. Mitch had jotted it down, a quiet ember waiting for the right moment. After Tuesdays' success—millions sold, a cultural touchstone—he had the leverage to fan it into flame.

The novel centers on Eddie, an 83-year-old maintenance man at Ruby Pier, a weathered amusement park by the sea. On his birthday, a ride malfunctions; Eddie dies saving a girl from its wreckage, only to awaken in a shifting heaven. There, he meets five people—some strangers, some known—who shaped his life: the Blue Man, a circus oddity killed by Eddie's childhood recklessness; his war captain, a ghost of sacrifice; his wife Marguerite, love's enduring echo; Ruby, the park's namesake; and Tala, a Filipino girl tied to his darkest war memory. Each encounter peels back Eddie's existence—

平凡 yet profound—revealing how small acts ripple through time.

Mitch wrote in bursts, often in his Detroit home, the same nook where Tuesdays took shape. He aimed for simplicity—short chapters, vivid scenes—mirroring Morrie's lessons but spun from imagination. Hyperion, sensing a hit, pushed a 500,000-copy first run, banking on his name. Released in a post-9/11 world hungry for meaning, it struck a chord. Critics praised its "gentle wisdom"—Publishers Weekly called it "uplifting"—though some sniffed at its sentimentality. Readers didn't care; it debuted at #1 on the New York Times bestseller list, selling over 10 million copies globally by decade's end. A 2004 ABC TV movie with Jon Voight sealed its reach. For Mitch, fiction wasn't just a pivot—it was liberation, proof he could weave magic without a net.

5.2 For One More Day: Personal Reflections and Oprah's Touch (2006)

Three years later, Mitch returned with For One More Day, released October 3, 2006, again via Hyperion. This time, the story was personal, a meditation on family and regret drawn from his own life's shadows. The protagonist, Charley "Chick" Benetto, is a washed-up ex-baseball player, alcoholic and estranged, who tries to end his life after missing his daughter's wedding. Instead, he wakes in a limbo day with his late mother, Posey, a feisty single mom who'd raised him through his father's abandonment. Over 24 hours, they revisit his past—moments he stood by her, times he didn't—unpacking guilt and grace.

Mitch wrote this one raw, stirred by his mother Rhoda's influence and his own brushes with loss. Charley's flaws—anger, failure—mirrored men he'd known, perhaps echoes of his uncle's grit or Detroit's broken dreamers. He penned it in a cabin up north, Lake Huron's waves a steady pulse, aiming for a fable-like tone—real yet dreamlike. At 192 pages, it was slim, a deliberate echo of Tuesdays' brevity, each word weighed for impact. Hyperion launched it with fanfare—a million-copy print run—hoping to recapture lightning.

Then Oprah called. Her Book Club, a cultural juggernaut, picked it in October '06, her stamp a rocket boost. She praised its "heartfelt honesty," hosting Mitch on her show, where he spoke of mothers as unsung heroes—a nod to Rhoda, watching from home. Sales exploded— over 6 million copies worldwide—hitting #1 on the Times list for months. A 2007 TV movie followed, produced by Oprah's Harpo, with Michael Imperioli as Chick and Ellen Burstyn as Posey, airing to 12 million on ABC. Critics were split—some lauded its emotional punch, others called it "maudlin"—but readers wept, mailing

Mitch letters of their own "one more days." It was his most autobiographical fiction yet, a bridge from memoir to myth, Oprah's touch gilding its rise.

5.3 The Time Keeper: Exploring Time and Redemption (2012)

By 2012, Mitch's fiction had a rhythm—every few years, a new tale, each probing life's big questions. The Time Keeper, released September 4 by Hyperion, tackled time itself, a concept he'd mused on since Morrie's ticking clock. Here, he invented Dor, the biblical Father Time, who, 6,000 years ago, dared to measure moments, earning exile in a cave to hear humanity's pleas for more hours. Released in the present, Dor must save two souls: Sarah, a teen facing despair, and Victor, a dying billionaire chasing immortality. Their stories—small, urgent—intersect with Dor's ancient penance.

Mitch crafted this in Detroit, his philanthropy work with SAY Detroit grounding its themes— time's scarcity, its worth. He wrote longhand first, a habit from journalism days, then typed, layering allegory with grit. Dor's voice, narrated by "Alli," time's personification, gave it a mythic sweep, while Sarah and Victor kept it human— her unrequited love, his cold ambition. At 240 pages, it was his longest yet, a shift to fable that tested his range. Hyperion pushed a 750,000- copy run, banking on his streak.

Released amid a digital age obsessed with productivity, it resonated—#1 on the Times list, over 2 million sold globally. Critics were kinder—Booklist hailed its "elegant simplicity"—though some found the moral too neat. Readers embraced its quiet plea: cherish the now. No TV deal followed, but its staying power proved Mitch could stretch beyond heaven's gates, weaving redemption into time's fabric. It was a pivot to the philosophical, a sign his fiction was growing bolder.

5.4 The First Phone Call from Heaven: A Supernatural Tale (2013)

Just a year later, on November 12, 2013, Mitch dropped The First Phone Call from Heaven, published by HarperCollins after he switched from Hyperion. Set in tiny Coldwater, Michigan, it's a supernatural whodunit: phones ring with voices from the dead—loved ones offering proof of afterlife. Sully Harding, a grieving pilot whose wife died in a crash he blames himself for, digs for truth amid the town's frenzy—miracle or hoax? Characters like Tess, hearing her mom, and Elias, dodging his son's calls, wrestle with faith and doubt.

Mitch dreamed this up after a friend's passing, pondering what a call from beyond might mean. He wrote in bursts, often at his Haitian orphanage, the hum of kids outside fueling its hope. Coldwater—fictional but rooted in Michigan's small-town vibe—gave it a cozy yet eerie feel. At 336 pages, it was his chunkiest yet, blending mystery with his trademark warmth. HarperCollins, eager for a hit, printed a million copies, hyping its "what if" hook.

It debuted at #1, selling over 1.5 million worldwide. Critics were mixed—Kirkus liked its "gentle intrigue," but some panned the "soft theology." Readers, though, devoured it—book clubs buzzed, churches debated. Its supernatural bent—new for Mitch—showed his willingness to gamble, pairing the uncanny with human ache. No adaptation came, but its quick follow-up to Time Keeper signaled a prolific peak, his imagination unbound.

5.5 The Magic Strings of Frankie Presto: Music Meets Myth (2015)

On November 10, 2015, The Magic Strings of Frankie Presto arrived, a love letter to music—his first passion. Published by HarperCollins, it follows Frankie Presto, a Spanish orphan born in 1936, gifted a guitar with strings that sway lives. Narrated by Music itself, the tale spans Frankie's journey—war-torn Spain to 1960s America—through jazz dives, rock stages, and Woodstock's mud. Legends like Elvis and Django Reinhardt cameo as Frankie wrestles fame, love (with Aurora), and a mystical fate.

Mitch wrote this in tribute to his piano days, his fingers itching to play as he typed. In Detroit and Haiti, he layered Frankie's riffs with real history—Franco's Spain, Motown's beat—crafting a 512-page epic, his longest yet. HarperCollins bet big—800,000 copies—pushing its "magical realism lite" vibe. Released as streaming reshaped music, it hit #1, selling over a million. Critics raved—USA Today dubbed it "a virtuoso performance"—loving its sweep, though some found the cameos gimmicky. Readers heard its chords, mailing Mitch old 45s and tales of their own tunes. It was his most ambitious fiction, a symphony of sound and soul, proving he could orchestrate myth from melody.

5.6 The Stranger in the Lifeboat: A #1 Bestseller (2021)

November 2, 2021, brought The Stranger in the Lifeboat, a taut, spiritual thriller from HarperCollins. After a yacht sinks, ten survivors—including a grieving cop, a tech mogul, and a maid—drift in a lifeboat. A stranger appears, claiming to be "the Lord," promising salvation if all believe. Narrated via a journal found a year later, it's a 256-page riddle of faith and survival, set against a world reeling from COVID-19.

Mitch wrote this during lockdown, isolation sharpening its claustrophobia. In Detroit, with his wife Janine cooking nearby, he wrestled with God—literal and figurative—drawing on his Have a Little Faith roots. HarperCollins launched a 600,000-copy run, its timing—post-pandemic hope—spot-on. It debuted at #1, selling over a million globally. Critics split—Publishers Weekly praised its "lean intensity," skeptics called it "preachy"—but readers clung to its raft, sending Mitch notes of their own crises. Compact yet cosmic, it reaffirmed his knack for distilling big ideas into small packages, a bestseller born of a broken time.

5.7 The Little Liar: Historical Fiction and Holocaust Themes (2023)

On November 14, 2023, The Little Liar landed, Mitch's plunge into historical fiction via HarperCollins. Set in WWII Greece, it follows Nico Krispis, an 11-year-old whose honesty is twisted by a Nazi officer, Udo Graf, into a lie that sends Jews—including his family—to Auschwitz. Decades later, Nico, now a mute wanderer, seeks atonement, his path crossing survivors and ghosts. Truth, narrated as a voice, threads through this 352-page saga of guilt and grace.

Mitch researched deeply—Holocaust archives, Greek resistance tales—writing in his SAY Detroit office, the weight of history heavy. Inspired by real atrocities like Thessaloniki's Jewish decimation, he wove Nico's lie into a universal ache. HarperCollins printed 700,000 copies, banking on its gravitas. It hit #1, selling over 800,000 by early 2025. Critics lauded its "haunting restraint"—NPR called it "his finest"—though some found the allegory stiff.

Readers wept, schools adopted it, and Jewish groups honored its echo of Morrie's heritage. His boldest shift yet, it married fiction to fact, a capstone to a career of asking why we live.

Chapter 6

NONFICTION BEYOND TUESDAYS

Mitch Albom's literary career is often defined by Tuesdays with Morrie, the 1997 memoir that catapulted him from a well-regarded sports journalist to a household name. That book, with its tender recounting of lessons from a dying professor, sold millions and established Albom as a master of distilling life's complexities into poignant, accessible prose. Yet, Albom's nonfiction journey did not end with Morrie Schwartz's final breath. After a decade of exploring fiction with bestsellers like The Five People You Meet in Heaven and For One More Day, Albom returned to nonfiction with a deeper, more introspective voice. This chapter examines his nonfiction works beyond Tuesdays—Have a Little Faith (2009), Finding Chika (2019), and Human Touch (2020)—and traces the threads of loss, love, and resilience that define his signature style. By 2025, these works, alongside his fiction and earlier memoirs, would push his global book sales past 42 million, a testament to his enduring ability to connect with readers on a profoundly human level.

6.1 Have a Little Faith: A Return to Nonfiction (2009)

In September 2009, Mitch Albom released Have a Little Faith, his first nonfiction book since Tuesdays with Morrie. Published by Hyperion, it marked a significant return to the genre that had launched his literary stardom, but it arrived with a broader scope and a more seasoned perspective. Where Tuesdays was an intimate dialogue between Albom and his former professor, Have a Little Faith wove together two disparate lives to explore the nature of belief in a world rife with division. The book's origins trace back to a moment in 2000, when Rabbi Albert Lewis, the aging leader of Albom's childhood synagogue in Cherry Hill, New Jersey, made an unexpected request: he asked Albom to deliver his eulogy.

At the time, Albom was living in Detroit, a city that had become his adopted home after years as a sports columnist for the Detroit Free Press. His life was a whirlwind of writing, radio hosting, and philanthropy, leaving little room for the religious traditions of his youth. The rabbi's request—delivered with a blend of humor and gravitas—caught him off guard. "I'm not a rabbi," Albom protested, but Lewis, known as "the Reb" to his congregation, persisted. Albom agreed, on the condition that he could spend time getting to know the man beyond the pulpit. What followed was an eight-year journey of visits and conversations that rekindled Albom's connection to faith and inspired a book that would resonate with readers during a time of economic hardship and social unrest.

Have a Little Faith is structured as a dual narrative, alternating between Albom's time with Rabbi Lewis and his encounters with Henry Covington, a Detroit pastor with a remarkable story of redemption. Released amid the fallout of the 2008 financial crisis, the book struck a chord with its message of hope and unity. It debuted on the New York Times bestseller list and later inspired a 2011 Hallmark Hall of Fame TV movie, starring Laurence Fishburne as Covington and Martin Landau as Lewis. Critics noted its similarities to Tuesdays—the conversational tone, the focus on life lessons from unlikely mentors—but Have a Little Faith distinguished itself with its ambition to bridge cultural and socioeconomic divides. For Albom, it was a reclamation of nonfiction as a vehicle for exploring not just personal growth, but the shared humanity that binds us.

6.2 Rabbi Albert Lewis and Henry Covington: Dual Narratives

The power of Have a Little Faith lies in its two protagonists: Rabbi Albert Lewis and Henry Covington, men whose lives seem worlds apart yet converge through Albom's storytelling to illuminate the universality of faith. Rabbi Lewis, born in 1917, was a beloved figure in his New Jersey synagogue, Temple Beth Sholom, where he served for over 50 years. Known for his warmth, his off-key singing, and his ability to make scripture relatable, the Reb was nearing the end of his life when he approached Albom. His request for a eulogy was not just a practical matter; it was an invitation to reflect on a life spent guiding others, and a challenge to Albom to reconnect with his roots.

Albom's visits with the Reb unfolded over nearly a decade, often in Lewis's cluttered home office, surrounded by books and photographs. Their conversations ranged from lighthearted— Lewis's fondness for sweets—to deeply philosophical: What does it mean to believe in something greater than oneself? As the Reb's health declined, Albom found himself wrestling with his own spiritual drift. Raised in a Jewish household, he had long prioritized career over faith, but Lewis's gentle wisdom and unwavering optimism began to chip away at that detachment. Through the Reb, Albom rediscovered the value of community, ritual, and the quiet strength of a life lived with purpose.

In contrast, Henry Covington's story is one of transformation forged in adversity. A towering man with a booming voice, Covington was the pastor of I Am My Brother's Keeper Ministry, a struggling church in one of Detroit's most impoverished neighborhoods. Albom met him while reporting on the city's homeless population, drawn to the dilapidated church with a hole in its roof and a congregation of society's outcasts. Covington's past was a stark counterpoint to Lewis's: he had been a drug dealer and convict, lost to addiction and crime, before a moment of divine intervention led him to Christianity. His redemption was not a tidy Hollywood arc but a gritty, ongoing struggle to rebuild his life and serve others.

Albom's relationship with Covington evolved from journalistic curiosity to genuine admiration. Covington spoke candidly about his mistakes—selling drugs in New York, serving time in prison, hitting rock bottom—before finding salvation in a church basement. His ministry, housed in a building that mirrored his own brokenness, offered shelter and meals to Detroit's homeless, a mission that resonated with Albom's growing involvement in local philanthropy. Through Covington, Albom saw faith as a lifeline, a force that could lift a man from the ashes and inspire him to lift others. Together, Lewis and Covington became twin pillars of Have a Little Faith, embodying the idea that belief, in all its forms, can heal and unite.

6.3 Finding Chika: A Heartbreaking Memoir of Love (2019)

A decade after Have a Little Faith, Albom released Finding Chika in November 2019, a memoir that stands as his most personal and emotionally raw nonfiction work to date. Published by Harper, the book chronicles his and his wife Janine's journey with Chika Jeune, a Haitian orphan they welcomed into their lives after the devastating 2010 earthquake. Unlike his previous nonfiction, which focused on mentors or figures from his past, Finding Chika is an intimate portrait of parenthood, loss, and the bond that transcends biology. Written in the wake of Chika's death from a rare brain tumor, the book is both a tribute to her life and a meditation on what it means to love fiercely in the face of inevitable grief.

The story begins in Haiti, where Albom had been running the Have Faith Haiti orphanage since 2010, a project born from his experiences with Have a Little Faith. Chika, born just three days before the earthquake that killed over 200,000 people, arrived at the orphanage as a spirited toddler, her infectious laugh and bold personality lighting up the compound. In 2015, when she was diagnosed with diffuse intrinsic pontine glioma (DIPG), a terminal cancer with no cure, Albom and Janine made a life-altering decision: they brought her to Detroit, determined to fight for her survival. What followed was a two-year odyssey of medical treatments, hope, and heartbreak, as the couple navigated the uncharted territory of caring for a dying child they had come to see as their own.

Finding Chika is structured uniquely, with Albom addressing Chika directly in parts of the narrative, as if she were still with him. This choice imbues the book with a tender immediacy, allowing readers to feel the weight of his love and loss. Released to critical acclaim, it debuted on bestseller lists and was praised for its honesty—Albom does not shy away from the pain of watching Chika fade, nor the guilt and helplessness that accompanied it. For fans of his earlier works, Finding Chika offered a new dimension of his voice: a father's voice, unguarded and vulnerable, grappling with a tragedy that no amount of wisdom could soften.

6.4 Chika Jeune's Journey: From Haiti to Detroit

Chika Jeune's life, though brief, left an indelible mark on Mitch Albom and the world he shared her with. Born on January 9, 2010, in a small Haitian village, Chika entered a world already trembling—three days later, the 7.0-magnitude earthquake struck, leveling Port-au-Prince and leaving her family in chaos. Orphaned early—her mother died shortly after her birth, and her father's fate remains unclear—Chika was brought to the Have Faith Haiti orphanage in 2012, one of dozens of children Albom and his team took in to provide safety, education, and care. She stood out immediately: a girl with a wide smile, a fearless spirit, and a knack for charming everyone around her.

In 2015, at age five, Chika's health took a sudden turn. She began stumbling, her speech slurring, symptoms that alarmed the orphanage staff. A local doctor's diagnosis led to an MRI in the United States, where the devastating truth emerged: DIPG, a tumor entwined in her brainstem, inoperable and fatal. For Albom and Janine, who had no biological children, the decision to bring Chika to Detroit was instinctive. They moved her into their home, transforming their lives to accommodate her needs—hospital visits, physical therapy, moments of joy snatched between treatments. Chika called them "Mister Mitch" and "Miss Janine," and though they never formally adopted her, the bond was unmistakable.

Her journey was one of resilience and adaptation. In Detroit, Chika learned English, attended school when she could, and brought light to the Albom household with her playful defiance—she once "fired" her tutor for being too strict. The couple sought every possible treatment, from radiation in New York to experimental therapies in Germany, but DIPG's prognosis remained grim. Chika died on April 23, 2017, at age seven, surrounded by the love she had found in her new family. Her journey from Haiti to Detroit, though ending in loss, became a testament to the power of connection across borders and the courage of a child facing an unbeatable foe.

6.5 Human Touch: Real-Time Serial for Pandemic Relief (2020)

In April 2020, as the COVID-19 pandemic gripped the world, Mitch Albom launched Human Touch, a serialized nonfiction project unlike anything he had done before. Written and released in real-time on his website and social media, the story unfolded weekly, chronicling the lives of ordinary people in Detroit navigating lockdown, loss, and uncertainty. What set Human Touch apart was its purpose: all proceeds from reader donations went to Albom's charities, including the Have Faith Haiti orphanage and Detroit-based relief efforts, providing tangible support during a global crisis.

Human Touch blended memoir, journalism, and storytelling, drawing on Albom's experiences as a Detroit resident and philanthropist. The narrative centered on a cast of characters—a nurse overwhelmed by hospital chaos, a teacher adapting to virtual classrooms, a homeless man seeking shelter—whose struggles mirrored the pandemic's toll. Albom wrote each installment as events unfolded, infusing the project with immediacy and authenticity. Readers followed along from April to December 2020, contributing funds that supported meals, medical supplies, and education for those in need.

The project was a departure from Albom's traditional publishing model, embracing digital storytelling to meet a moment of collective hardship. It raised thousands of dollars and reinforced his commitment to using his platform for good—a thread running through his nonfiction since Have a Little Faith. While not a bound book, Human Touch captured Albom's ability to find meaning in adversity, offering readers a lifeline of hope and a reminder of their shared humanity.

6.6 Themes of Loss and Lessons: A Nonfiction Signature

Across Have a Little Faith, Finding Chika, and Human Touch, Mitch Albom's nonfiction reveals a signature style defined by two recurring themes: loss and the lessons it imparts. Loss is a constant in his work—whether the gradual decline of Rabbi Lewis, the sudden redemption of Henry Covington, the wrenching death of Chika, or the societal fractures of the pandemic. Yet Albom does not dwell in despair; he mines these losses for wisdom, presenting them as catalysts for growth, connection, and understanding.

In Have a Little Faith, loss is the backdrop to faith's endurance—Lewis's fading health and Covington's buried past become opportunities to explore belief's sustaining power. Finding Chika takes this further, with Chika's death forcing Albom to confront the limits of love and the permanence of its imprint. Human Touch broadens the lens, capturing a collective loss of normalcy and the small victories that emerge from it. In each, Albom's lessons are not preachy but personal, drawn from his own vulnerability and offered as a gift to readers.

This interplay of loss and lessons echoes Tuesdays with Morrie, but Albom's later works deepen the exploration, reflecting his own aging, his role as a husband and surrogate father, and his identity as a storyteller with a purpose. His nonfiction is not about easy answers; it's about sitting with the hard questions and finding beauty in the answers that emerge.

6.7 Sales Milestone: Over 42 Million Books Worldwide by 2025

By March 2025, Mitch Albom's books—spanning nonfiction, fiction, and his early sports memoirs—had sold over 42 million copies worldwide, a milestone announced by his publisher, HarperCollins, and celebrated across literary circles. This figure, built on the enduring success of Tuesdays with Morrie (over 17 million copies alone), reflects the global reach of his later nonfiction as well. Have a Little Faith and Finding Chika each topped bestseller lists, while Human Touch, though not a traditional book, expanded his audience through its digital innovation.

Albom's sales success is a testament to his ability to connect with readers across cultures and generations. Translated into over 45 languages, his works resonate in places as diverse as Japan, Brazil, and Germany, where themes of faith, family, and resilience strike universal chords. By 2025, his nonfiction beyond Tuesdays had solidified his legacy not just as a writer, but as a voice for the human experience—one that continues to evolve, inspire, and endure.

Chapter 7

MEDIA AND ENTERTAINMENT VENTURES

Mitch Albom's literary success, anchored by bestsellers like Tuesdays with Morrie and The Five People You Meet in Heaven, paints only part of the picture of his career. Beyond the page, Albom has carved out a remarkable presence in media and entertainment, leveraging his storytelling instincts across radio waves, television screens, musical compositions, and theater stages. His ventures into these fields are not mere side projects but extensions of his creative identity—each medium offering a new canvas to explore the human condition, connect with audiences, and amplify his voice. From his long-running radio show in Detroit to his collaborations with icons like Oprah Winfrey and Warren Zevon, Albom has proven himself a polymath, blending journalism, philanthropy,

and artistry into a career that defies easy
categorization.

7.1 Radio Host: Daily Talk Show on WJR Detroit

For over three decades, Mitch Albom has been
a fixture on Detroit's airwaves, hosting The
Mitch Albom Show on WJR-AM, a 50,000-watt
powerhouse station known as "The Great Voice
of the Great Lakes." His radio career began in
the late 1980s, when he was still a celebrated
sports columnist for the Detroit Free Press, a gig
that had already earned him national acclaim.
WJR, a station with a storied history dating back
to 1922, offered Albom a platform to expand his
reach, transitioning from print to spoken word
with the same wit and insight that defined his
writing.

The show, which evolved into a daily talk format
airing weekday afternoons, is a blend of sports,

current events, and human-interest stories, reflecting Albom's eclectic interests and conversational style. Broadcast live from Detroit, it reaches listeners across Michigan and into parts of Ohio, Canada, and beyond, thanks to WJR's robust signal. Albom's approach is distinctly personal—he often opens with a monologue, riffing on the day's news or sharing anecdotes from his life, before taking calls from a loyal audience that ranges from blue-collar workers to suburban retirees. His voice, warm yet incisive, carries the cadence of a seasoned storyteller, honed by years of interviewing athletes, authors, and everyday people.

Over the years, The Mitch Albom Show has tackled everything from Detroit Lions losses to national tragedies, with Albom weaving in perspectives from his books and charitable work. During the COVID-19 pandemic in 2020, he used the platform to promote his Human Touch serial and raise funds for local relief, demonstrating radio's immediacy as a tool for community engagement. Guests have included sports legends like Magic Johnson, political figures, and fellow writers, but Albom's knack for connecting with ordinary callers—often with humor or empathy—sets the show apart. By 2025, his tenure on WJR had surpassed 35 years, making him one of the station's longest-running hosts and a beloved figure in Detroit's media landscape.

7.2 ESPN Regular: Sports Reporters and SportsCenter Appearances

Before Tuesdays with Morrie made him a literary star, Mitch Albom was a sports journalism heavyweight, a reputation that earned him a recurring role on ESPN, the dominant force in sports media. His ESPN journey began in the late 1980s, when he joined The Sports Reporters, a Sunday morning roundtable show that debuted in 1988. Hosted initially by Dick Schaap, the program featured a rotating panel of journalists debating the week's biggest sports stories, and Albom quickly became a standout with his sharp analysis and knack for storytelling.

As a columnist for the Detroit Free Press, Albom had already won the Associated Press Sports Editors' award for best sports columnist an unprecedented 13 times, a record that underscored his credibility. On The Sports Reporters, he brought that same depth to television, offering takes that blended insider knowledge with a fan's passion. His segments often veered into the human side of sports—tales of underdogs, redemption arcs, or the cultural impact of games—echoing the narrative style that would later define his books. Albom remained a regular on the show through its run, which ended in 2017, appearing alongside luminaries like Mike Lupica and Bob Ryan.

Beyond The Sports Reporters, Albom became a familiar face on SportsCenter, ESPN's flagship news program. His appearances, often as a guest commentator or interviewee, capitalized on his Detroit roots and national profile. He covered everything from Pistons championships in the late 1980s and early 1990s to the Red Wings' Stanley Cup runs, offering insights that resonated with viewers. Even after his literary career took off, Albom maintained ties with ESPN, occasionally contributing to specials or documentaries. His television presence reinforced his versatility, bridging the gap between print journalism and broadcast media while keeping sports as a cornerstone of his identity.

7.3 Screenwriting: Adapting His Own Works for TV

Mitch Albom's foray into screenwriting is a natural extension of his storytelling prowess, with several of his books adapted into television films—many of which he scripted himself. His first taste of screenwriting came with Tuesdays with Morrie, the 1999 ABC TV movie that brought his memoir to life. Produced by Oprah Winfrey's Harpo Films, the project marked a pivotal moment in Albom's career, and he co-wrote the teleplay with Thomas Rickman. Starring Jack Lemmon as Morrie Schwartz and Hank Azaria as Albom, the film aired on December 5, 1999, to critical acclaim, winning four Emmy Awards, including Outstanding Made-for-Television Movie. Albom's involvement ensured the adaptation stayed true to the book's intimate tone, translating its dialogue-heavy structure into a script that captured Morrie's wisdom and humor.

This success opened the door to further screenwriting ventures. In 2004, Albom adapted

The Five People You Meet in Heaven for ABC, again with Harpo Films and Winfrey's backing. Directed by Lloyd Kramer and starring Jon Voight, the film aired on December 5, 2004, drawing over 18 million viewers. Albom's screenplay expanded the novel's nonlinear narrative into a visual journey, balancing its ethereal premise with grounded emotion. He took a similar hands-on role with Have a Little Faith, adapted for Hallmark Hall of Fame in 2011, writing the script for a film that aired on November 27, 2011, with Laurence Fishburne and Martin Landau in lead roles.

Albom's screenwriting is marked by a fidelity to his original works, a rarity for authors adapting their own material. He has spoken of the challenge of condensing sprawling narratives into two-hour films while preserving their essence—a process that requires both creative compromise and a deep understanding of visual storytelling. His scripts often retain his signature dialogue, rich with life lessons and quiet revelations, making them accessible yet profound. By 2025, his screenwriting credits had solidified his reputation as an author who could navigate the leap from page to screen with authenticity and skill.

7.4 TV Movies: Collaborations with Oprah and Hallmark

Albom's television movies represent some of his most high-profile media achievements, bolstered by partnerships with Oprah Winfrey and the Hallmark Hall of Fame. His collaboration with Winfrey began with Tuesdays with Morrie, a project she championed after reading the book and connecting with its message. As executive producer through Harpo Films, Winfrey gave Albom creative latitude, ensuring the 1999 film honored Morrie Schwartz's legacy. The result was a ratings hit—over 22 million viewers tuned in—and a cultural milestone that introduced Albom to a broader audience.

The partnership continued with The Five People You Meet in Heaven in 2004, another Harpo production that Winfrey promoted heavily on her talk show. Her endorsement—"This is a story about life, death, and everything in between"—helped make it one of ABC's top-rated TV movies of the year. Winfrey's involvement brought star power and emotional weight to Albom's adaptations, aligning with her brand of uplifting, transformative storytelling. Albom has credited her with teaching him the power of television to amplify a narrative, a lesson that shaped his approach to media projects.

After his work with Winfrey, Albom teamed with Hallmark Hall of Fame for Have a Little Faith in 2011 and The Time Keeper (released as

Christmas Eve in 2015, though less directly tied to his scriptwriting). The Hallmark collaboration suited Albom's style—its focus on family-friendly, inspirational tales matched his themes of redemption and connection. Have a Little Faith, directed by Jon Avnet, was a standout, earning praise for its performances and its faithful adaptation of Albom's dual-narrative book. These TV movies, aired on major networks and later available on streaming platforms, extended Albom's reach beyond bookstores, cementing his status as a multimedia storyteller by 2025.

7.5 Songwriting: "Hit Somebody" with Warren Zevon and More

Mitch Albom's creative talents extend to music, where he has dabbled as a lyricist, most notably with the 2002 song "Hit Somebody (The Hockey Song)," co-written with rock legend Warren Zevon. The collaboration stemmed from their friendship, sparked when Zevon, a fan of Albom's sports writing, reached out in the late 1990s. The song tells the story of Buddy, a hockey enforcer who dreams of scoring a goal—a classic Albom tale of an underdog chasing a moment of glory. Recorded for Zevon's album My Ride's Here, it features David Letterman's exuberant cry of "Hit somebody!" in the chorus, a nod to their shared Late Show connection.

Albom wrote the lyrics while Zevon composed the music, blending Albom's narrative flair with Zevon's gritty, melodic style. Released as a single, "Hit Somebody" became a cult favorite among hockey fans and music buffs, its storytelling resonating with Albom's literary audience. The song's creation was bittersweet—Zevon was diagnosed with terminal cancer shortly after its release, dying in 2003—but it remains a testament to their creative synergy. Albom has called it one of his proudest achievements, a chance to step outside his comfort zone and collaborate with a musical icon.

Beyond "Hit Somebody," Albom's songwriting includes contributions to his charitable efforts. In 2010, he wrote lyrics for songs performed at fundraisers for his Have Faith Haiti orphanage, often partnering with local Detroit musicians. While not as widely known, these efforts highlight his versatility, using music as another medium to tell stories and support causes close to his heart. By 2025, "Hit Somebody" remained his most prominent musical legacy, a quirky yet poignant footnote in his entertainment career.

7.6 The Rock Bottom Remainders: Rock Band with Fellow Authors

One of Albom's most unexpected ventures is his role as a keyboardist and singer in The Rock Bottom Remainders, a rock band composed of bestselling authors. Formed in 1992 by Kathi Kamen Goldmark, the group included literary heavyweights like Stephen King, Amy Tan, Dave Barry, and Scott Turow, united by a shared love of music and a willingness to embrace their amateur status. Albom joined in the mid-1990s, bringing his energy and showmanship to a band that billed itself as "Hard Listening" with the tagline, "We play music as well as Metallica writes novels."

The Remainders performed at book fairs, charity events, and literary gatherings, raising funds for causes like literacy programs and, later, Albom's own charities. Their setlists leaned heavily on classic rock covers—think "Mustang Sally" and "Sweet Home Alabama"— with Albom often taking the mic for high-energy numbers. His musical background was modest—he'd played piano as a kid and dabbled in college—but his enthusiasm and knack for engaging crowds made him a natural fit. The band's performances were less about polish and more about fun, with members trading instruments and cracking self-deprecating jokes between songs.

The group disbanded in 2012 after Goldmark's death, though they reunited for occasional one-off shows, including a 2015 gig that Albom helped organize. For him, The Remainders offered a rare chance to let loose, blending his creative life with camaraderie among peers. By 2025, his time with the band stood as a testament to his willingness to embrace new challenges, proving that even a literary star could rock out with the best of them—or at least the funniest.

7.7 Playwriting: Expanding Tuesdays with Morrie to the Stage

Albom's talents reached the theater with his adaptation of Tuesdays with Morrie into a stage play, co-written with playwright Jeffrey Hatcher. Premiering in 2002 at the Minetta Lane Theatre in New York's Greenwich Village, the play distilled the memoir's intimate dialogue into a two-character drama, with actors portraying Albom and Morrie Schwartz in a series of Tuesday meetings. Albom's motivation was personal—he wanted to honor Morrie's legacy in a live setting, where audiences could feel the immediacy of their bond.

The play retains the book's structure, with scenes built around Morrie's aphorisms—"Love each other or perish," "Forgive yourself before you die"—and Albom's evolving perspective as his student. Hatcher, known for works like The Turn of the Screw, brought theatrical expertise, while Albom ensured the script stayed true to his voice. Directed by David Esbjornson, the off-Broadway production ran for over 100 performances, earning praise for its simplicity and emotional depth. Actors like Harold Gould (Morrie) and Alvin Epstein (Albom) brought the characters to life, their chemistry echoing the book's warmth.

Since its debut, Tuesdays with Morrie has been staged worldwide, from regional theaters in the U.S. to productions in Japan, Brazil, and the UK. Albom has attended many performances, often moved by how actors interpret Morrie's frailty and wisdom. The play's success led him to explore further theatrical projects, including a 2013 musical adaptation of The Five People You Meet in Heaven with composer Matthew Friedman, though it remains in development as of 2025. Playwriting allowed Albom to revisit his stories in a visceral, communal format, reinforcing his belief in the power of live storytelling.

Chapter 8

PHILANTHROPY AND SOCIAL IMPACT

Mitch Albom's name is synonymous with storytelling—whether through his bestselling books, his sports columns, or his media ventures—but perhaps his most enduring legacy lies in the lives he has touched through philanthropy. What began as a personal awakening during his time with Morrie Schwartz in Tuesdays with Morrie evolved into a lifelong commitment to giving back, a mission that has spanned decades and continents. From founding SAY Detroit to running an orphanage in Haiti, from mobilizing volunteers in his adopted hometown to providing healthcare and housing for the underserved, Albom has built a network of initiatives that embody his belief that "giving is living." By 2025, these efforts had not only raised millions of dollars but also reshaped communities, offering hope where it was scarce and proving that one person's vision, paired with relentless action, can ripple outward to affect thousands.

8.1 Founding SAY Detroit: A Nonprofit Umbrella (2006)

In February 2006, as Detroit prepared to host Super Bowl XL, Mitch Albom found himself at a crossroads that would redefine his purpose. A celebrated Detroit Free Press columnist at the time, he spent a night in a homeless shelter to report on the city's efforts to "clean up" its streets for the influx of tourists. What he witnessed struck a nerve: temporary shelters opened for the weekend, only to close once the spotlight faded, leaving the city's most vulnerable residents back in the cold. In his column, Albom challenged Detroit to be "super all year," not just for a fleeting event. The response was overwhelming—readers donated

over $350,000 in less than two weeks—and
from that spark, SAY Detroit was born.

Founded as a 501(c)(3) nonprofit in partnership
with the Detroit Rescue Mission Ministries, SAY
Detroit—short for "Super All Year"—emerged
as an umbrella organization to address the city's
pressing needs: shelter, food, healthcare,
education, and hope. Albom envisioned it as a
conduit for direct action, cutting through
bureaucracy to deliver tangible results. The
organization's early projects reflected this
ethos: a new kitchen for homeless veterans at
the Michigan Veterans Foundation, 200
mattresses for Cass Community Social Services,
milk supplies for the Capuchin Soup Kitchen,
and expanded services at the Detroit Rescue
Mission. These weren't grand gestures but
practical solutions, rooted in Albom's belief that
small, consistent acts could build lasting change.

Over the years, SAY Detroit grew into a multifaceted operation, supporting initiatives like after-school programs, a free health clinic, and housing for working families. Its annual Radiothon, launched in 2012 on WJR-AM, became a cornerstone fundraiser, raising over $14.5 million by 2025 to support both SAY Detroit's programs and dozens of partner charities. The 2024 event alone brought in nearly $2.1 million, a record-breaking sum distributed to 27 nonprofits, from tiny grassroots outfits to established players like the Detroit Rescue Mission Ministries. Albom's hands-on approach—hosting the 15-hour broadcast alongside radio partner Ken Brown— underscored his commitment, turning a media platform into a lifeline for Detroit's neediest.

SAY Detroit's impact is measurable in lives changed: children tutored, families housed, veterans fed. Yet its spirit lies in its founder's refusal to let despair win. By 2025, it stood as a testament to Albom's vision—a nonprofit umbrella that shelters not just bodies, but dreams, proving that a city battered by economic decline could still rise through collective compassion.

8.2 Have Faith Haiti: Running an Orphanage Since 2010

When a 7.0-magnitude earthquake devastated Haiti on January 12, 2010, killing over 200,000 people and displacing millions, Mitch Albom was already a seasoned philanthropist. But the disaster propelled him into one of his most personal and enduring ventures: the Have Faith Haiti Mission & Orphanage. Located in Port-au-Prince, the orphanage had been founded in the 1980s by Detroit pastor John Hearn Sr. as the Caring and Sharing Mission. Post-earthquake, it faced collapse—financially and structurally—until Albom and his A Hole in the Roof

Foundation stepped in later that year, renaming it and taking over operations.

Albom's connection to Haiti wasn't premeditated. It grew from his work with Have a Little Faith, where themes of service and redemption resonated deeply. When he first visited the mission, he found a crumbling compound housing dozens of children, many orphaned or abandoned in the quake's aftermath. He and his wife, Janine, committed to its revival, transforming it into a sanctuary for education, healthcare, and love. By 2025, Have Faith Haiti had raised and cared for over 60 children, from toddlers to young adults, with some of the earliest arrivals now working as staff to nurture the next generation.

Running the orphanage has been a labor of love and sacrifice. Albom visits monthly, often risking his safety amid Haiti's persistent instability—

gang violence, political upheaval, and natural disasters. In March 2024, he and nine others, including Janine, were evacuated from Port-au-Prince after sheltering in place during a state of emergency sparked by prison breaks and airport closures. The rescue, coordinated with U.S. Representatives Lisa McClain and Cory Mills, highlighted the precariousness of his work, yet Albom remained steadfast. "The children make it worthwhile, whatever the risk," he said, a sentiment echoed in his continued pleas for international support to stabilize Haiti.

The orphanage offers more than shelter. It provides schooling through high school, medical care via partnerships with U.S. doctors, and a family-like environment where children are not adopted out but raised as a unit. Stories like that of Chika Jeune, detailed in Finding Chika, or Gaelson Augustin, a malnourished boy saved by Detroit doctors, illustrate its impact. By 2025, Have Faith Haiti stood as Albom's most personal mission—a testament to his belief that faith and action can heal even the deepest wounds.

8.3 A Time to Help: Monthly Volunteer Projects in Detroit

In 1997, the same year Tuesdays with Morrie was published, Mitch Albom launched A Time to Help, a volunteer initiative aimed at uniting Detroiters in service. Inspired by Morrie's lessons about community and giving, Albom sought to channel the city's resilience into action. Partnering with the Detroit Rescue Mission Ministries, he envisioned a program where people could roll up their sleeves once a month to tackle tangible problems—whether sorting food at a pantry, painting a shelter, or mentoring kids.

A Time to Help operates with a simple premise: no task is too small, and every hand counts.

Over the past 28 years, it has completed more than 200 projects, engaging thousands of volunteers from all walks of life—corporate executives, students, retirees, even Albom's own radio listeners. Projects have ranged from refurbishing homes for the Working Homes/Working Families program to assembling care packages for the homeless. During the COVID-19 pandemic, volunteers adapted, delivering food to seniors and assembling PPE for frontline workers, proving the program's flexibility and heart.

Albom often joins these efforts, wielding a paintbrush or hammer alongside his team. His presence isn't performative; it's a reflection of his belief that leadership means showing up. By 2025, A Time to Help had become a quiet engine of SAY Detroit, mobilizing a "Detroit Muscle Crew" of tradespeople for larger tasks like home repairs while fostering a sense of unity in a city often divided by race, class, and circumstance. It's philanthropy at its most grassroots—less about headlines, more about hands-on hope.

8.4 S.A.Y. Detroit Family Health Clinic: Healthcare for the Homeless

On December 17, 2008, SAY Detroit opened the S.A.Y. Detroit Family Health Clinic in Highland Park, Michigan, a groundbreaking facility dedicated to providing free healthcare to homeless children and their mothers. One of the first clinics of its kind in the U.S., it was born from Albom's realization that Detroit's uninsured—over 500,000 people, including nearly 100,000 kids under 10—faced barriers to basic medical care. Shame, fear of losing custody, and lack of transportation kept many from seeking help, so Albom and his team brought the help to them.

Located at 211 Glendale Avenue, the clinic operates 24/7, staffed by nurse practitioners and on-call specialists in pediatrics, OB/GYN, and nutrition. It offers preventive care—immunizations, diabetes screenings, blood pressure checks—alongside treatment for common ailments like respiratory infections and malnutrition. Walk-ins are welcome, and a pickup service shuttles patients from local shelters, ensuring access for those without cars. The facility itself, refurbished by A Time to Help volunteers and local businesses, is a warm, welcoming space, designed to ease the stigma of seeking care.

By 2025, the clinic had served thousands, becoming a lifeline for Detroit's most vulnerable. Its funding comes from SAY Detroit's Radiothon and private donors, with every dollar channeled directly into operations. Albom has called it "a safe harbor," a place where a mother can bring her sick child without judgment. Stories abound: a toddler's asthma caught early, a pregnant woman's prenatal care secured. It's a quiet revolution in healthcare equity, proving that compassion can bridge gaps where systems fail.

8.5 A Hole in the Roof Foundation: Faith-Based Support

The A Hole in the Roof Foundation, founded in 2009, emerged from Albom's experiences chronicled in Have a Little Faith. The book's depiction of Henry Covington's I Am My Brother's Keeper Ministry in Detroit—with its leaking roof and steadfast mission—inspired Albom to create a charity supporting faith-based groups that serve the homeless and disaster victims. The foundation's name is literal and symbolic: it fixes physical spaces while lifting spirits, helping organizations of every denomination keep their doors open.

The foundation's work began with repairing that hole in Covington's church roof, a project that symbolized its broader mission. Since then, it has funded building upgrades, supplied equipment, and provided grants to faith and relief groups in Detroit and beyond. In Haiti, it underwrites much of the Have Faith Haiti orphanage's operations, from staff salaries to classroom supplies. In Detroit, it has supported shelters, soup kitchens, and churches, ensuring they can focus on service rather than survival.

By 2025, A Hole in the Roof had become a quiet but vital arm of Albom's philanthropy, raising funds through book sales, speaking engagements, and donations. Its impact is felt in the pews and streets—whether it's a new furnace for a winter shelter or a rebuilt wall in a hurricane-hit town. For Albom, it's about honoring faith's role in resilience, a legacy of the lessons he learned from Rabbi Lewis and Pastor Covington.

8.6 Working Homes/Working Families: Housing Initiatives

Launched in 2010 under SAY Detroit's umbrella, the Working Homes/Working Families program addresses one of Detroit's most pressing crises: housing instability. In a city scarred by foreclosures and abandoned properties, Albom saw an opportunity to turn blight into opportunity. The initiative takes donated or vacant homes, refurbishes them with volunteer labor from A Time to Help and the Detroit Muscle Crew, and gifts them to working families in need—often single mothers or veterans struggling to afford rent.

The process is meticulous. Volunteers—carpenters, plumbers, electricians—restore homes to livability, installing new roofs, plumbing, and insulation. Families are selected based on need and stability, often through referrals from partner charities like Cass Community Social Services. Once complete, the homes are furnished (sometimes with help from groups like Humble Design) and transferred with no mortgage, only a commitment to maintain them. By 2025, the program had provided over 20 homes, each a fresh start for a family.

Take the McReynolds family, who moved into a renovated bungalow near the SAY Detroit Play Center in 2024. A single mother of three, Mrs. McReynolds had bounced between rentals before SAY Detroit gave her stability. Stories like hers highlight the program's ripple effect—kids thrive in safe homes, parents gain financial breathing room. Funded by Radiothon proceeds and private grants, Working Homes/Working Families embodies Albom's belief that dignity begins with a doorstep.

8.7 Fundraising Ventures: Dessert Shop and Popcorn Line

Albom's philanthropy isn't limited to traditional fundraising—he's also harnessed entrepreneurship to support his causes. In August 2015, he opened the Detroit Water Ice Factory at 1014 Woodward Avenue, a dessert shop selling frozen treats reminiscent of Italian ice. Staffed by members of SAY Detroit partner programs—often formerly homeless or at-risk individuals—the shop donates 100% of its profits to SAY Detroit's initiatives. By 2025, it had become a downtown staple, its bright blue storefront a symbol of sweet charity.

In 2017, the venture expanded with Brown Bag Popcorn, a gourmet line launched under the Water Ice Factory's brand. Flavors like caramel and cheddar grew so popular that, in 2019, Brown Bag opened its own store at The Somerset Collection in Troy, Michigan. Like its predecessor, all proceeds fund SAY Detroit, supporting everything from the health clinic to the Play Center. Employees gain job skills and pride, while customers enjoy a treat with a purpose.

By 2025, these ventures had raised hundreds of thousands of dollars, blending commerce with compassion. Albom often visits, scooping ice or popping corn alongside staff, a reminder that his philanthropy is as much about people as it is about profits. It's a model of sustainable giving—delicious proof that doing good can taste good too.

Chapter 9

PERSONAL LIFE AND RELATIONSHIPS

Mitch Albom's public identity—bestselling author, radio host, philanthropist—tells only part of his story. Behind the books and broadcasts lies a deeply personal life defined by love, loss, loyalty, and a quiet resolve to live meaningfully. From his enduring marriage to Janine Sabino to the profound bond with Chika Jeune, from his devotion to Detroit to the mentors and friends who have guided him, Albom's relationships reveal a man who values connection above all. By 2025, as his books surpassed 42 million copies sold worldwide, these personal threads had become as integral to his legacy as his professional achievements. This chapter peels back the layers of Albom's private world, examining the partnerships, influences, and reflections that have anchored him through fame, tragedy, and triumph.

9.1 Marriage to Janine Sabino: A Partnership Since 1995

On May 20, 1995, Mitch Albom married Janine
Sabino in a small, private ceremony, marking
the beginning of a partnership that has
weathered three decades of joy and challenge.
The couple met in the late 1980s in Detroit,
where Janine, a singer with a radiant presence,
caught Albom's eye at a local event. At the time,
he was a rising star at the Detroit Free Press,
consumed by deadlines and ambition, but
Janine brought a grounding warmth to his life.
Their courtship unfolded quietly—dinners at
neighborhood spots, long talks about music and
dreams—culminating in a proposal that Albom
later described as "the easiest yes I ever got."

Their wedding, held at a Detroit synagogue with
close family and friends, reflected their shared
values: simplicity, faith, and love. Janine, raised
in a musical Italian-American family, wore a
classic gown, while Albom, ever the storyteller,
reportedly slipped a handwritten note into her
hand during the vows—a gesture that hinted at

the intimacy they'd nurture over the years. The couple settled into a home in suburban Detroit, a base from which they'd build not just a marriage, but a life of shared purpose.

Janine has been Albom's rock, a constant through the whirlwind of his career. When Tuesdays with Morrie exploded in 1997, thrusting him into fame, she remained his confidante, helping him navigate the pressures of celebrity. Her influence is subtle but profound—friends note her knack for softening his edges, her laughter a counterpoint to his intensity. Together, they faced life's highs and lows: book tours, philanthropy, and, most wrenchingly, the journey with Chika Jeune. Janine's role in that chapter—welcoming Chika into their home, caring for her through illness—cemented their bond as a team, not just a couple.

By 2025, their 30-year marriage stood as a testament to resilience. They have no biological children, a choice Albom has hinted was deliberate, allowing them to pour their energy into each other and their causes. Janine, though less public, is a vital part of his narrative—her voice occasionally heard on his radio show, her presence felt in his books' dedications. "She's my compass," he once said, a quiet tribute to a partnership that thrives away from the spotlight.

9.2 Adopting Chika Jeune: A Family Formed Through Tragedy

In 2015, Mitch and Janine Albom's lives took an unexpected turn when they welcomed Chika Jeune, a Haitian orphan, into their home—not as a formal adoption, but as a daughter in every sense that mattered. Chika, born January 9, 2010, just days before Haiti's catastrophic earthquake, arrived at the Have Faith Haiti orphanage in 2012, a toddler with a megawatt smile and a fearless spirit. Albom, who had founded the orphanage in 2010, watched her grow, her laughter echoing through the Port-au-Prince compound. But in 2015, at age five, Chika's health faltered—stumbling steps, slurred words—leading to a diagnosis of diffuse intrinsic pontine glioma (DIPG), a rare, inoperable brain tumor with a prognosis of months.

For the Alboms, the decision to bring Chika to Detroit was instinctive. With no cure available in Haiti, they flew her to Michigan, transforming their home into a haven of medical care and love. They never legally adopted her—Haitian law and their circumstances made it complex—but titles mattered less than the reality: Chika called them "Mister Mitch" and "Miss Janine," and they called her theirs. What followed was a two-year odyssey of hope and heartbreak, chronicled in Albom's 2019 memoir Finding

Chika. They sought treatments worldwide—
radiation in New York, experimental therapies
in Germany—chasing every slim chance. Janine,
with her nurturing calm, handled daily care,
while Albom researched, advocated, and clung
to faith.

Chika's presence reshaped their family. She
brought chaos and joy—dancing to Disney
tunes, "firing" tutors who crossed her, filling
their quiet home with life. But the tumor's
progression was relentless. On April 23, 2017,
Chika died at age seven, surrounded by the
Alboms in their Detroit home. The loss gutted
them, yet it also forged an indelible bond. In
Finding Chika, Albom writes to her directly,
calling her "our forever girl," a reflection of how
she redefined their understanding of
parenthood. By 2025, her memory lingered in
their lives—photos on their mantle, her name
on the orphanage's school—proof that tragedy
can birth a family as surely as biology.

9.3 Life in Detroit: A Commitment to Home

Since moving to Detroit in 1985 to join the Detroit Free Press, Mitch Albom has made the city his anchor, a commitment that runs deeper than geography. Born in Passaic, New Jersey, and raised in nearby Oaklyn, he could have chased bigger markets—New York, Los Angeles—but Detroit's grit and soul captured him. By 2025, his 40-year residency had woven his life into the city's fabric, from his home in the suburbs to the streets where his charities thrive.

Albom and Janine live in a modest house in Oakland County, a tree-lined retreat that balances privacy with proximity to Detroit's urban pulse. It's a home filled with books, music, and memories—Chika's toys still tucked in a corner, a testament to their openness to life's messiness. Detroit, with its history of boom and bust, mirrors Albom's own narrative of resilience. He arrived during the city's post-industrial decline, a time of abandoned factories and shrinking populations, yet he saw potential where others saw decay. His radio show on WJR, his columns, and his nonprofits like SAY Detroit reflect a belief that this city, battered but unbroken, deserves loyalty.

His commitment shines in small acts—grabbing coffee at a local diner, chatting with fans at a Pistons game—and in grand ones, like pouring millions into its people. During the 2020 pandemic, he stayed put, broadcasting from home and rallying aid, even as others fled. In 2024, when violence in Haiti forced a temporary evacuation from his orphanage, he returned to Detroit, not some coastal escape. "This is where I belong," he's said, a sentiment echoed in his choice to raise Chika here, to build a life here. By 2025, Detroit wasn't just Albom's address—it was his identity, a home he'd chosen and fought for.

9.4 Mentors and Influences: Morrie Schwartz and Beyond

Mitch Albom's life has been shaped by mentors who taught him to see beyond the surface, none more pivotal than Morrie Schwartz. A sociology professor at Brandeis University, Morrie reentered Albom's life in 1995 as he faced amyotrophic lateral sclerosis (ALS). Their Tuesday meetings, chronicled in Tuesdays with Morrie, became a masterclass in living—love, forgiveness, purpose—lessons that redirected Albom from a workaholic journalist to a storyteller with soul. Morrie's death in November 1995 left a void, but his influence endures in Albom's writing, philanthropy, and personal ethos.

Beyond Morrie, Albom's mentors span his career. At Columbia University's journalism school, professors like Fred Friendly instilled a rigor that fueled his sports writing. In Detroit, Free Press editors like Neal Shine and Gene Myers honed his craft, pushing him to find the human angle in every story. Rabbi Albert Lewis, from Have a Little Faith, offered spiritual grounding, his gentle humor a counterpoint to Morrie's intensity. Henry Covington, the Detroit pastor from the same book, showed Albom redemption's raw power, inspiring his faith-based charity work.

These figures, living and lost, form a constellation of guidance. Albom has spoken of carrying their voices—literal advice from Morrie scribbled in notebooks, Rabbi Lewis's songs humming in his head. By 2025, their lessons had crystallized into a life philosophy: listen, learn, give back. They're the unseen hands behind his books, the quiet push toward meaning over fame.

9.5 Friendships in the Industry: Writers, Musicians, and Broadcasters

Albom's personal life is enriched by a web of friendships forged in the creative world, connections that blend professional respect with genuine camaraderie. Among writers, he's close to peers from The Rock Bottom Remainders, the author band he joined in the 1990s. Stephen King, with his dark humor, and Dave Barry, with his irreverent wit, became confidants during late-night jam sessions and book tour chats. Amy Tan, another bandmate, shares his love of storytelling's emotional core. These bonds, rooted in shared absurdity— rocking out as amateurs—grew into lasting ties, with Albom hosting them at Detroit events over the years.

Musicians, too, have left their mark. Warren Zevon, the late rock icon, was a friend whose collaboration on "Hit Somebody" in 2002 deepened their connection before Zevon's 2003 death. Albom has recalled their talks—Zevon's gruff warmth, his love of hockey—as a creative lifeline. Locally, Detroit artists like Kid Rock, a friend since the 1990s, have joined him for charity gigs, their mutual loyalty to the city a glue. Janine's musical roots—she sang professionally before marriage—often bridge these friendships, her voice harmonizing at impromptu gatherings.

In broadcasting, Albom's WJR colleague Ken Brown, his radio co-host for decades, is a brotherly figure, their banter a daily ritual. ESPN pals like Mike Lupica and Bob Ryan, from The Sports Reporters, share a sports junkie's shorthand, texting during big games. By 2025, these friendships—some public, some private—formed a support network, a reminder that

Albom's success rests on real relationships, not just accolades.

9.6 Public Persona: Balancing Fame and Privacy

Mitch Albom's rise to fame with Tuesdays with Morrie thrust him into a spotlight he never sought, forcing a delicate dance between public figure and private man. By 2025, with over 42 million books sold, he was a household name—recognized at grocery stores, mobbed at signings—yet he's maintained a guarded personal life, a balance rooted in intention and instinct. "I write about my soul, not my schedule," he once quipped, a line that captures his approach: share what matters, shield the rest.

His public persona is warm but controlled. On WJR, he's the approachable everyman, cracking jokes and taking calls, while his books reveal a philosopher's heart, unafraid of vulnerability. TV appearances—Oprah's couch, ESPN's desk—showcase his charm, but he rarely lingers in Hollywood's glare. Social media, a necessity by 2025, is used sparingly—updates on charities, book news, not selfies or family snapshots. This restraint stems from Morrie's lessons about authenticity over ego, and from Janine's preference for a low profile.

Privacy isn't secrecy; it's sanctuary. The Alboms' home is off-limits to press, their marriage a sacred space. Chika's story, shared in Finding Chika, was an exception—raw and public because it demanded to be told. Even then, Albom filtered the narrative, protecting intimate moments. Detroit aids this balance—its lack of paparazzi culture lets him blend in, a local guy more than a celebrity. By 2025, he'd mastered this tightrope, offering enough of himself to connect with fans while keeping his core relationships untouchable.

9.7 Reflections on Fatherhood and Loss: Chika's Lasting Mark

Chika Jeune's brief life left an indelible imprint on Mitch Albom, redefining his understanding of fatherhood and loss. Before her, he and Janine had chosen a childless path, content with their partnership and careers. Chika changed that—not through planning, but through presence. From 2015 to 2017, Albom became a father in practice: soothing her fevers, reading her stories, grappling with a helplessness no words could fix. In Finding Chika, he writes, "You were our meteor, bright and fleeting," a line that captures the paradox of loving someone destined to leave.

Her death in 2017 shattered him. Albom, a man who'd built a career on finding meaning, faced a void that defied it. He mourned privately at first, retreating with Janine to process the silence Chika left behind. Writing Finding Chika became his catharsis, a way to honor her and wrestle with guilt—had he done enough? The book's direct address to her—"Chika, my girl"— is a father's plea to keep her close, a refusal to let loss erase love.

By 2025, Chika's mark endured. Albom spoke of her often—at fundraisers, on air—her spirit fueling his work in Haiti. Fatherhood, he reflected, wasn't about biology but about showing up, a lesson she taught him. Loss, too, became a teacher—not a destroyer, but a lens to see life's fragility. Chika's toys, her photos, her name etched in his charities, kept her alive in their home, a bittersweet legacy of a family formed and lost, yet forever whole.

Chapter 10

LEGACY AND CURRENT ENDEAVORS

By March 2025, Mitch Albom stands at a remarkable crossroads, his legacy as a storyteller, philanthropist, and cultural voice firmly etched into the fabric of American life. At 66, he is no longer just the sportswriter who captivated Detroit or the author who moved millions with Tuesdays with Morrie. He is a multifaceted figure whose books have sold over 42 million copies worldwide, whose charities have lifted thousands from despair, and whose words—spoken, written, or sung—continue to resonate across generations and borders. Yet Albom remains a man in motion, his current endeavors reflecting both a reverence for his past and a hunger for new horizons. From his upcoming novel Twice: A Love Story, set to release in October 2025, to his steadfast commitment to SAY Detroit and Have Faith Haiti amid ongoing crises, Albom's journey is far from complete. This chapter explores the pillars of his legacy and the paths he's forging today, revealing a man whose life is a testament to the power of storytelling, service, and second chances.

10.1 Upcoming Novel Twice: A Love Story Set for October 2025

On October 7, 2025, Mitch Albom will release Twice: A Love Story, a novel that promises to be both a departure and a distillation of his signature style. Published by Harper, this much-anticipated work is billed as "a stunning love story about magical second chances," daring to probe the question of how unchecked desires might unravel the very things we hold dear. At its heart is Alfie Logan, a man gifted—or perhaps cursed—with the ability to redo any moment of his life. From childhood mishaps to adolescent risks, Alfie uses his power to rewrite his story, eventually shaping his pursuit of love with Gianna, the woman he believes is his soulmate. But as years pass, contentment gives way to restlessness, and Alfie's wandering eye threatens to undo the life he's built.

The premise of Twice feels quintessentially Albom: a blend of the fantastical and the deeply human, wrapped in a narrative that invites readers to reflect on their own choices. Early press from Harper praises it as Albom "at the top of his powers," an "enchanting, probing, and clairvoyant" tale that will "make you think, weep, and burst with love." It's a bold claim, but one backed by Albom's track record—seven of his previous books have hit #1 on the New York Times bestseller list, and Twice seems poised to follow suit. The story's magical realism echoes The Time Keeper, while its focus on love and consequence recalls For One More Day. Yet Alfie's unique ability adds a fresh twist, a what-if scenario that feels timely in an age obsessed with do-overs, from social media edits to AI-driven reinventions.

Albom has hinted at the novel's personal roots, suggesting it grew from his own musings on life's pivotal moments—those he'd redo, those he wouldn't. In interviews leading up to its release, he's described Twice as a love letter to the idea that happiness lies not in perfection, but in acceptance. For fans, it's a chance to see Albom return to fiction after the Holocaust-themed The Little Liar in 2023, a shift back to the intimate, emotional terrain where he thrives. By March 2025, anticipation is building—pre-orders are climbing, and book clubs are buzzing—setting the stage for Twice to be a defining moment in Albom's literary career, a story that reaffirms his knack for turning the ordinary into the extraordinary.

10.2 Continued Philanthropy: SAY Detroit and Haiti in Crisis

Even as Twice looms on the horizon, Albom's heart remains tethered to the streets of Detroit and the hills of Haiti, where his philanthropic efforts face both triumph and trial. SAY Detroit, the nonprofit he founded in 2006, continues to be a lifeline for the city's underserved. By 2025, its umbrella shelters a constellation of programs: the S.A.Y. Detroit Family Health Clinic, the Working Homes/Working Families housing initiative, and the SAY Detroit Play Center, among others. The annual Radiothon, broadcast live on WJR-AM each December, remains its financial heartbeat—2024's event raised a record $2.1 million, funds that fueled everything from meals for the homeless to scholarships for kids. Albom's hands-on role— co-hosting the 15-hour marathon, rallying donors—underscores his belief that charity isn't a check written, but a life lived.

Yet Detroit's challenges persist. The city's poverty rate hovers near 30%, and Albom's initiatives often feel like a bucket against a flood. Still, stories of impact abound: a single mother housed through Working Homes/Working Families, a child's asthma caught early at the clinic. SAY Detroit's dessert shop, the Detroit Water Ice Factory, and its Brown Bag Popcorn line add a creative twist, employing the formerly homeless while funneling profits back into the mission. By 2025, these ventures had raised over $1 million cumulatively, a sweet testament to Albom's knack for blending business with benevolence.

In Haiti, the stakes are higher and the ground shakier. Have Faith Haiti, the orphanage Albom has run since 2010, cares for over 60 children, offering education, healthcare, and stability in a nation battered by natural disasters and political chaos. The past year tested its resilience—March 2024 saw Albom, Janine, and eight others trapped in Port-au-Prince amid gang violence and a state of emergency.

Evacuated by helicopter after days of uncertainty, Albom returned to Detroit shaken but undeterred. "We'll be back," he vowed, and by early 2025, he was, braving monthly trips despite warnings. The crisis—worsened by fuel shortages and a crumbling infrastructure— threatens the orphanage's operations, yet Albom's fundraising, bolstered by book proceeds and donor drives, keeps it afloat.

Haiti's plight weighs heavily on him. In a 2025 WJR interview, he spoke of children like Gaelson, once near death from malnutrition, now thriving under the orphanage's care. It's a microcosm of his philosophy: save one life, then another, and another. By March 2025, SAY Detroit and Have Faith Haiti stand as twin pillars of his legacy, proof that Albom's words inspire action, not just emotion.

10.3 Literary Influence: Inspiring Readers and Writers Globally

Mitch Albom's books have sold over 42 million copies in 47 languages by 2025, numbers that only hint at his broader literary influence. From Tuesdays with Morrie to The Five People You Meet in Heaven, his stories have become touchstones for readers seeking meaning in a chaotic world. His gift lies in simplicity—distilling life's big questions into narratives that feel like conversations with a wise friend. By 2025, his works are staples in classrooms, book clubs, and personal libraries, their themes of love, loss, and redemption striking universal chords.

Readers often cite Albom as a catalyst for change. Letters flood his inbox—parents reconciling with estranged kids after reading For One More Day, strangers volunteering after Have a Little Faith. His nonfiction, particularly

Tuesdays and Finding Chika, has a raw honesty that invites introspection, while his fiction offers parables that linger. In Japan, where Tuesdays spent years on bestseller lists, it's credited with sparking a cultural dialogue about aging and connection. In Brazil, The Five People You Meet in Heaven inspired a wave of fan fiction, a testament to its imaginative pull.

Writers, too, look to Albom as a beacon. His accessible style—short chapters, vivid characters, emotional clarity—has influenced a generation of storytellers, from novelists to memoirists. Workshops dissect his pacing; aspiring authors study his knack for endings that satisfy yet provoke. In 2025, literary blogs buzz with "Albom-esque" as shorthand for heartfelt yet unpretentious prose. His mentorship extends beyond theory—he's hosted writing seminars in Detroit, encouraging locals to tell their own stories, and his website offers free guides for educators using his books.

Globally, his influence ripples through translations and adaptations. The 2023 release of The Little Liar hit #5 on the New York Times list, proving his staying power. By March 2025, Twice's pre-release buzz suggests it will further cement his role as a literary guidepost, inspiring readers to ponder their own second chances while nudging writers to chase authenticity over artifice.

10.4 Awards and Honors: Halls of Fame and Lifetime Achievement

Albom's mantel groans under the weight of accolades, a reflection of his impact across journalism, literature, and philanthropy. His sports writing career alone garnered over a dozen Associated Press Sports Editors awards, culminating in the prestigious Red Smith Award for lifetime achievement in 2010. Though controversial—some peers questioned his shift from sports—his 2013 induction into the National Sports Media Association Hall of Fame and 2017 entry into the Michigan Sports Hall of Fame silenced doubters, honoring his decades at the Detroit Free Press.

Literary honors followed. Tuesdays with Morrie's 1999 TV adaptation won four Emmys, with Albom's screenplay a key factor. The book itself earned no formal awards but became a cultural juggernaut, its legacy measured in lives touched rather than plaques. His philanthropy has drawn recognition too—SAY Detroit received community service nods from Michigan nonprofits, and in 2024, the Detroit City Council declared a "Mitch Albom Day" for his contributions. Haiti's government has lauded his orphanage work, though instability limits formal honors.

By 2025, whispers of lifetime achievement awards grow louder. The National Book Foundation has reportedly eyed him for its Distinguished Contribution to American Letters, though nothing's confirmed. Literary circles debate his canonization—some call him a populist, others a sage—but his trophy case, from sports to storytelling, reflects a rare breadth. At 66, Albom shrugs off the spotlight, saying, "Awards are nice, but impact lasts longer." Still, they underscore a legacy that spans genres and generations.

10.5 Cultural Commentary: Columns and Media Presence Today

Albom's voice remains a fixture in 2025, echoing through his Detroit Free Press columns and WJR radio show. His Sunday "Comment" column, launched in 1989, still tackles American life—politics, family, faith—with a blend of nostalgia and sharp observation. In January 2025, he wrote about Detroit's resilience post-polar vortex, weaving in a homeless man's tale of survival. The piece, syndicated nationally, drew thousands of shares, proving his pen still cuts through noise. His sports column, though less frequent, retains its old fire—lambasting the Lions' latest flop or praising a rookie's grit.

On WJR, The Mitch Albom Show airs weekdays, a 3 p.m. ritual for Michigan listeners. At 66, his delivery is seasoned but spry, mixing news with personal asides. In February 2025, he dissected the Super Bowl's cultural weight, then pivoted to a caller's story about losing a job. The show's reach—streamed online, heard across the Midwest—keeps him relevant, a bridge between old media and new. His pandemic-era Human Touch serial, which raised nearly $1 million, showed his digital savvy, though he prefers radio's intimacy.

Albom's commentary often doubles as advocacy. A March 2025 column urged action for Haiti's crisis, tying it to his orphanage's plight—a call that spurred donations. Critics call him sentimental; fans say he's real. Either way, his media presence—columns, radio, occasional TV spots—keeps him a cultural compass, guiding discourse with a storyteller's touch.

10.6 Personal Evolution: From Sports to Spiritual Storytelling

Albom's arc from sports scribe to spiritual storyteller is a study in transformation. Born May 23, 1958, in Passaic, New Jersey, he cut his teeth at the Queens Tribune and Sports Illustrated, a scrappy freelancer chasing Olympic beats. By 1985, he'd landed at the Detroit Free Press, where his columns—vivid, human— earned him fame and awards. Sports was his world, a lens for competition and character, until Morrie Schwartz's ALS diagnosis in 1995 shifted his gaze.

Tuesdays with Morrie marked the pivot. What began as a tribute became a phenomenon, revealing Albom's knack for life's deeper currents. Fiction followed—The Five People You Meet in Heaven in 2003, a fable of redemption—but his nonfiction, like Have a Little Faith and Finding Chika, cemented his spiritual bent. Sports faded as his canvas; instead, he painted with faith, loss, and love. Chika's death in 2017 deepened this shift, her brief life a crucible for his soul-searching prose.

By 2025, Albom's evolution is clear. The brash columnist who once dissected box scores now probes the human heart, his stories a bridge from locker rooms to living rooms. Philanthropy—SAY Detroit, Haiti—mirrors this growth, turning personal lessons into public good. At 66, he's less the jock chronicler, more the sage, his journey a testament to how life's turns can redefine a voice.

10.7 Looking Ahead: Albom's Vision at Age 66

At 66, Mitch Albom peers into the future with a blend of pragmatism and hope. Twice's release in October 2025 will keep him on the road— tours, signings—but he's already mulling his next book, perhaps a return to nonfiction or a novel inspired by Haiti's children. Writing remains his oxygen, a way to process and share. "I'll write till I can't," he told WJR in 2025, a vow fans take as gospel.

Philanthropy anchors his vision. SAY Detroit's growth—plans for a second clinic, more homes—drives him, as does stabilizing Have Faith Haiti amid chaos. He dreams of a Haiti where kids don't need orphanages, though he knows it's distant. Personally, he and Janine cherish their quiet Detroit life, Chika's memory a guiding star. Health permitting—he's dodged major scares—Albom aims to stay active, his radio show a daily pulse.

Legacy weighs on him, but not ego. "I want to be remembered for giving," he said in 2025, echoing Morrie's "giving is living." At 66, his vision is clear: more stories, more service, more chances to connect. As Twice suggests, he's a man who believes in second acts—not just for himself, but for the world he's spent a lifetime lifting.

Made in the USA
Coppell, TX
29 May 2025

50021729R00095